Emotional Memoirs
& Short Stories

Lani Hall Alpert

Book design by Lani Hall Alpert, Gerry Wersh, and Chris Adjani
Photography by Lani Hall Alpert
Author Photograph by Maryanne Bilham
Edited by Kelly Sanchez and Eric Bemiller

Published in the United States by Lani Hall Alpert.

ISBN 978-1479206285

Printed in the United States of America

www.lanihallalpert.com

DEDICATION

This book is dedicated to my husband, Herb Alpert. My home is in his arms. He is perfect kindness. Words cannot approach the murmurs of my heart. He is my song. Wherever he is… I am home.

To my blessings, Aria, Chris, Eden, Dore, and Ellen. And my 5 grandchildren, Aarron, Emily, Kylie, Duke, and Miles.

To my beloved brother, Richard Hall, whose love and support is a constant blessing in my life.

To my mother and father, Mary and Peter Hall. Always in my heart.

To Benita Argis, who was my teacher as well as my friend.

And to Chicago, the city that lives inside of me.

ACKNOWLEDGEMENTS

I would like to thank the following people for their encouragement, patience, time spent, comments, and support during the many incarnations of this book.

My husband, Herb Alpert, for his love and ever-present friendship and support. Your creative soul is a constant inspiration and your love is a light that guides me.

Gerry Wersh, for his generous help, patience and invaluable creative ideas for anything placed in front of him.

Chris Adjani, for his personal and professional effort, creativity, and honesty and his endless ideas and willingness to help.

Kevin Almeida for his help, availability and thoroughness in proof reading and research, and continuously making it better.

My precious daughter, Aria, whose love and truthfulness I will always depend on.

My brother, Richard Hall, who gives me his focus, attention and acceptance with honesty and love.

Milton Kahn for his belief and enthusiasm.

Steve Fisher for forging ahead and being so available.

Jim Gosnell for his open willingness to help.

Kay Cessna, who has been a nurturing source in so many ways.

Rona Sebastian for encouraging me with her open heart, loving enthusiasm and friendship.

Caroline Graham for her giving spirit.

Jay Weston for his meaningful emails and his honesty.

Bill Moyers, for his soulful presence.

To the following people whose loving friendship and support gives me strength: Ellen Wolff Wimmer, Mimi Feldman, Susan Wunderlich, Page and Lou Adler, Jerry and Ani Moss, Sergio and Gracinha Mendes, Rick and Irit Ehrlich, Ted and Tammy Feigin, and Terry Robinson. And to all those who rallied behind me to go forward with this book.

CONTENTS

4

CONTENTS

Emotional Memoirs
& Short Stories

Emotional Memoirs

It's the light I remember most when I go back to Chicago. Forgotten memories are sparked by the light. The slow-moving clouds, and the shadows they cast, paint a mystery where none had been before. My emotions change with the light, catapulting me back to a different time. A different era.

Tall city buildings stretch and breathe, reflecting colors and the movements of the sky in their mirror-like windows. The sun's rays brighten the ground, while clouds, dark and full of moisture, backdrop the green foliage that soaks up the golden heat like a Van Gogh dance. There is an aliveness to the light. An excitement. My eyes would widen with awe and anticipation at the descending force from the green, thunderstorm clouds. I could almost hear music when the sun backlit their ragged edges.

In winter the trees were stripped of their fullness, exposed like skeletons silhouetted against the relentless gray sky. Everyone's eyes looked down so as not to slip on icy sidewalks while puffs of delicate condensation emanated from their mouths as they breathed hard from the hard winters.

I'd come home to a rush of radiator heat and wait for my fingers and face to thaw so that I could sing. I was a closet singer back then. I just wanted to sing for the sole sake of expressing myself. I'd hold the handle of a hairbrush as a microphone, and then I'd close my eyes and sing with my records. I'd sing all kinds of music, but jazz was my favorite.

My neighbor Jackie was the only other person who shared my love for jazz. She had a great record collection that we listened to together. She was also my safety net when things got bad at home. Jackie was 11 years older than me and was married and had a little boy that I babysat for. We shared the same back porch, where we'd usually bump in to one another.

COME RAIN OR COME SHINE

I watched him as he stood in the summer heat, his hands resting on the gray wooden railing of our shared porch. He was always in his jockey shorts, and was the first man I'd ever seen almost naked. He was lean and smooth, and I imagined he was strong by the way his muscles rippled on the sides of his arms.

I'd say, "Hi, Frank," and he would look at me unfazed, not embarrassed at all to be standing in his underwear in front of a 12-year-old girl. "Hi," he'd answer. Then, opening the screen door to his kitchen, he'd walk back to his little boy and his wife, Jackie. He walked kind of like Paul Newman in *The Hustler*.

I liked Frank. He was from Hell's Kitchen in New York City. I liked anything that was from New York, but I really liked the accent. It was tough and standoffish. It made me want to find the gentleness behind that rough edge.

Frank was funny in a put-down kind of way, and bright enough to know that his marriage wasn't working and that maybe he shouldn't have married the girl he'd knocked up. But it was too late for those thoughts. His three-year-old son Joey was in their apartment clinging to his mommy's leg, already feeling the insecurities of bitter parents.

Not to say that Jackie and Frank didn't love each other. I thought they did even when I would hear them fighting on those hot summer nights when everyone left their screen doors open. Their arguments were always pretty heated, but nothing as bad as the fights between my mom and dad.

A year passed. It was 1959, and I hadn't seen much of Jackie and Frank. Then Jackie asked my mom if I could babysit for Joey. My older brother used to babysit before he joined the Air Force. I guess she figured now that I was a teenager I was more responsible. It was also convenient, since we lived right next door to each other, and shared the same back porch.

It was the night I started babysitting that I discovered that Jackie and Frank had separated and he had gone back to New York. It disturbed me to think that I might never again see Frank standing on the porch in his jockey shorts, and that two people could make a decision not to live together when they were married and had a kid. On the other hand, there was something modern and adventurous about Jackie and Frank, so I accepted it, but I did get the feeling from Jackie that it was only temporary.

Jackie was cool. She even smoked "Kool" cigarettes, and every other word that came out of her mouth was slang. When she wrote to Frank, she would write on the envelope "Fly it," instead of "Air Mail." Her painted fingernails curved down like the claws of a cat, and the only music she ever played was jazz.

After school I'd rush to Jackie's apartment and we'd laugh and play jazz and order cheese pizza from around the corner. When the doorbell rang, she'd glide dance across the room in a way that made her feet look as if they never left the floor. Answering the door in an unbuttoned trench coat with a half-slip pulled over her bare breasts, she'd joke with the delivery boys. Everyone liked Jackie.

The only ones who didn't like her were my parents. They thought she was a bad influence on me, but all of my friends' parents thought I was a bad influence on them, so it didn't matter much to me. There were nightly fights at my house about money or school or things I didn't understand. It was hard for me to breathe there.

Whenever I had trouble at home, I would run out the back door and down the porch steps that connected to a maze of back porches that led to Joey's bedroom window. I would climb in and enter Jackie's apartment so that my parents wouldn't see me go in from the porch. It was my sanctuary. It gave me time and relief. My parents could never understand the freedom I felt at Jackie's. I could be myself there and at the same time be part of Jackie's exciting world, which was nothing like the colorless life my parents lived in.

Sometimes I would sing for Jackie. She loved it when I sang "The Man That Got Away" from the *Judy Garland at Carnegie Hall* album. I would stand in the middle of her living room and sing my heart out, and she would cry and tell me what a wonderful singer I was. She made me feel like I was on stage at Carnegie Hall. She was my friend. Even though she was 24 and I was 13.

Jackie got a job working as a waitress at a bar by the lakefront, and I started babysitting for Joey almost every night. I'd go over early just to watch her get ready. She had talent as an artist, and it showed in the way she put on her makeup. She would outline her dark eyes with sweeping strokes of black pencil and apply her lipstick so that it was just above her natural lip line to make her lips appear fuller. She would tease her jet-black hair until it bubbled out, and put on her push-up brassiere, and wear full skirts to hide her full hips. Then she'd slide on her ebony-framed cat eye shaped glasses and go to work.

Jackie met Tom about a month after she started working. I was sleeping on the couch when I heard her laugh and then some whispering. "Who's that on the couch?" Tom asked as he came over to shake me awake. He was handsome and had a warm smile. I liked him. I rubbed my eyes and walked out the back door to go home, but as I was leaving, something in Jackie's laugh told me that Tom was staying.

Jackie's king-sized bed sat in the middle of her converted dining room and was visible from almost anywhere in her apartment. Joey had the only bedroom, so Jackie's affair with Tom had to be when Joey was sleeping.

I kind of knew they were sleeping together, but didn't really know what that meant. I didn't know anything about sex, but I did learn about romance from the movies. I tried to be "hip" like Jackie so I wouldn't ask too many questions; I didn't want her to think I was a "square." She didn't reveal too much about Tom and her, except that they had a lot of fun together and that she liked him.

He shook me awake, and in my dreamy state, I said, "Hi, Tom." A soft, deep voice answered, "Hi, I'm Rick." My eyes focused, and in the dim lamp glow his light blue eyes pierced through me. His hair was the color of dark sand, and kind smile lines were etched in his ivory skin. He was beautiful. Tall and lean, a little like Frank, but there was something delicate about him, and at the same time something quietly intense. Jackie was also quiet. Her laugh silenced by her hunger for Rick.

Jackie and Rick were an instant couple. She talked about him constantly, and they were always together. She told me how he would hold her in his arms and roll his tongue all around her mouth when they kissed. Their song was "Come Rain or Come Shine" by Ray Charles, and they played it all the time. The tempo of the music changed too. Now a steamier and slower jazz spilled from her apartment windows.

Rick would usually wait for Jackie at the bar, and they would wake me when they came home. One night I was sleeping on the couch, and was awakened by their voices. They were in the bathroom, and Rick was saying that he didn't love her anymore and he wanted to leave. She wept uncontrollably, then suddenly stopped. As I walked slowly to the porch I could hear the sound of muffled whispers and splashing bathwater. I thought it was so beautiful to be that close to someone, so in love, as if they belonged together.

I wanted to be like that with someone. I wanted to listen to jazz and smoke "Kool" cigarettes and go to nightclubs and be "hip" and glide dance and wear push-up brassieres and makeup. Sometimes, while Joey was sleeping, I would go through Jackie's drawers and try on her lingerie and watch myself in the mirror while I played jazz and polished my fingernails. Everything felt so different and alive at Jackie's. I felt grown-up and special there.

Even though I saw so much of Rick, I never really knew what to say to him. I was a little bashful, since I knew such intimacies about their relationship. And then there was his beauty. He was beautiful to look at, and listen to. He had a mystery and a dark pain about him. It was elusive. I didn't understand it. All I knew was that Jackie loved him.

Once Rick came over before Jackie got home, and for some reason he threw me, fully dressed, into the bathtub and turned on the water. As he lifted me out of the tub, with my wet clothes on, I put my arms around his neck and imagined what it must be like for Jackie to hold him. It was a playful scene. The only one I ever had with him.

It wasn't long after that I learned about Rick's darkness. Rick was a junkie. He mainlined heroin. He had been in and out of jail because of his habit. Jackie assured me that she hadn't known about it in the beginning, but now she was so much in love with him that it didn't seem to matter. She had made Rick promise to never use drugs in front of either one of us, and Jackie and I swore to each other that we would never try them. She told me that if she ever caught me trying any kind of drug she would skin me alive.

She was telling me this because I was her friend. She seemed nervous as she spoke, but somehow it didn't shock me. In fact, it was more exciting now. The music, the language, the erratic behavior all brought a new meaning to the songs on the record player. I would go to school singing Lambert, Hendricks & Ross bebop songs while everyone else was playing Frankie Avalon. I'd say "man" and call a car a "short." I was a beatnik. I loved being different. There was a secret thrill to my life. An added dimension. It was cool.

Everyone dropped out of Jackie's life except for Rick and me. Jackie even took advantage of Frank's letters longing for his son and sent Joey to New York to be with him for a while. Now, Rick's friends suddenly found a safe haven to shoot drugs. When Jackie was gone, Rick would leave the back porch door open, and Jimmy and Sam and Paulie and other nameless men would drift into her kitchen to shoot up and then wander back to the streets again and again. I would see them coming and going like quiet shadows, but oddly enough, my parents and the neighbors never seemed to notice them.

I went to Jackie's apartment even when she was gone. One day, a friend of mine unexpectedly came there to tell me that Jackie was getting a bad reputation, and that I shouldn't spend so much time at her apartment. Then she saw the junkies in the kitchen and ran out horrified and very angry with me. What was wrong with her? It was hip! She just didn't understand. She was like all of my other friends, blind to life beyond high school. But not me. I knew a language that she couldn't understand. I knew about lovers and jazz. I knew about raw and real life.

I bumped into Sam on the street one day. "Don't ever use drugs, not ever," he said to me. He was hunched over, his eyes drooping, slowly pointing his finger at me in a weak yet scolding gesture. He was dead serious. I felt that he cared about me. On that street corner, midday, this sad soul was telling me something important. I listened to him and said, "Don't worry, I won't," and then I ran off to Jackie's.

She was crying. Knees bent, legs curled up on her turquoise plastic couch. "Rick's busted," she said. I knew it meant he'd been arrested. He was going to jail for six months for drug possession. Six months. It sounded like an eternity.

I spent a lot of time waiting with Jackie. She needed me now. It was grueling. She wrote love letters to Rick, but she wouldn't read them to me. She said that they made love to each other in their letters. I thought it was beautiful, and I felt her longing and loneliness. I counted the days with her and tried to make her laugh. We ordered pizza from around the corner and took the bus to the Riviera Theatre to see the latest movies. I slept over sometimes when she felt her loneliest, but mostly stayed until she wanted to go to sleep. Then I would cross the porch and go home.

The letters kept her going, and the junkies, with their mannerisms, reminded her of Rick. She kept them around, nodding on her couch, listening to jazz, shuffling in and out at all hours until the day he arrived. Rick was coming home, and Jackie's skin was crawling with excitement. I didn't see much of them, but I thought about them all the time. Once in a while, Jackie and I would meet on the porch for a few minutes and she'd tell me how wonderful it was to be sleeping with him again. Then she'd rush back to him, promising to tell me more later on.

It was August 1, 1961. I was 15. Two weeks had passed since Rick was back, and Jackie woke up with a terrible toothache. Her dentist could only see her in the late afternoon, and after her appointment she went shopping for dinner and got home late.

I thought it was strange when she telephoned, frantically asking to speak to my dad. I wondered why she was phoning when she could have simply crossed the porch. My father's face was still. Moments after he hung up, Jackie was standing at my screen door. It felt awkward as she entered our kitchen. I was always in her kitchen. I don't remember Jackie ever being in our apartment. As she came in, my father passed silently and crossed the porch.

"Jackie, what is it?" I asked.

Her face was pale with fear, and her eyes darted around the room as she bit her fingers. With a choking voice she answered, "I think Rick's dead."

I grabbed her by the shoulders and screamed in her face, "No! No, he's not! He couldn't be!" She looked so frightened, and I tried to calm her. "It's okay, don't worry. It's going to be fine," I assured her. I didn't believe for one moment that Rick was dead. Not for an instant. I knew that a love as strong as theirs would last forever.

When my father returned, the look on his face brought a stinging doubt to my heart. He went to the phone to call the police. Through all of my family's difficult and troubled times I still trusted my father. I asked. "Is he dead? Dad, is he?" I searched his eyes for a crack of light, but the darkness was too thick. He hesitated at first, and then his words sent me spinning. "I think so."

I ran out the back door and crossed the porch to Jackie's kitchen and walked slowly toward the dining room. There, on the king-sized bed, in the lamplight glow from the living room, Rick was lying on his back. I moved closer, saying his name softly. The closer I moved, the louder I spoke, until I was shouting his name. The bed was neatly made. I didn't notice anything out of place. It was so quiet in the room that all I could hear was my own beating heart pounding loudly. It was the first time I had ever seen Rick with his eyes closed, but I could still see their steel blue color in my mind. He was wearing dark trousers and a white shirt that had been pulled open. Then I noticed his ear. It was turning green.

In the middle of my head I heard a high-pitched ring that made me dizzy. I covered my ears with my hands and rushed out the back door. I looked up at the starry sky and prayed to whatever had taken Rick to please take me instead. "They love each other," I cried. "They need each other. Please, please, take me instead."

I was standing on the same porch that Frank had stood on in his jockey shorts. The same porch the junkies used to get to Jackie's kitchen. I raced down the gray wooden steps saying, "No, don't. Please don't do this." I ran down the alley, down blocks and blocks of dark streets to my friend who was angry with me for letting the junkies use Jackie's kitchen. She was the only friend I had that knew about Jackie. Gasping for air, between deep sobs, I told her what had happened, but she couldn't say anything. How could I expect her to understand? No one could understand. The sun had just lost all of its light and heat. Now everything was dark. And cold.

I wanted to go far away, but I found myself walking in the courtyard of my building. Looking up at Jackie's window I saw her pacing back and forth, crying and pacing and, it seemed, waiting for me. I stayed with her that night, not knowing what to do or say. I felt numb, as though I were dreaming.

The next morning Jackie's doorbell rang. Two policemen stood in the doorway asking if she knew Rick. "Did you mail these letters to him while he was in jail?" And there it was, right in front of her. A tied bundle. All of her passion on paper. She stared at it silently until they interrupted her memory. "You're under arrest for sending lewd material through the mail."

My legs started to shake. Jackie choked back her tears and lashed out with anger. "See that bed? Rick died there last night of a drug overdose, and you're telling me I'm under arrest?"

Shock covered their faces and the room filled with silence. They quietly apologized and left the letters with her. I thought it was kind of them to be so understanding. Jackie crumbled.

Rick's mother and Jackie were the only two people at Rick's funeral. There was a chapel service at Barr Funeral Home on Lawrence Avenue and then the burial. Jackie didn't want me to go.

Rumor had it that when Jackie left for the dentist, after promising her that he was shaking his habit, Rick called his drug connection. Maybe he shot too much, or an air bubble hit his vein, or his tolerance went down after being in jail for half a year. His dealer tried to save him, but it was too late. I remember asking the junkies in the neighborhood where I could find Rick's dealer. I wanted to kill him. In my mind I took out all my rage on him and the thought of finding him, but I never did.

Jackie was destroyed. She didn't know what to do with her life. She looked so lost and alone. I didn't know what to do, so I just stayed with her. It seemed as if she needed to connect with someone who really knew her, and out of desperation she wrote to Frank. Of course, she never wrote anything about Rick, but I'm sure he sensed her terrible loneliness.

The whole month after Rick died, Jackie prayed that she was pregnant so that he would still be alive inside of her. It was the only hope that kept her going. But it wasn't meant to be, and her sadness tripled. The junkies dwindled down. Jimmy and Paulie were the only two who came around. The music was bluer. Jimmy would sit on the couch till three or four in the morning pretending to listen to the music, but he was really nodding from the drugs. I would watch him in the dim radio light. He looked pathetic sitting there, his eyes half closed, slowly moving his head up and down, mumbling to himself. Jackie hid the Ray Charles album so that no one would accidentally play "Come Rain or Come Shine." It would have been too much for her to bear.

The colors were fading fast. The excitement was leaving my blood, and a strange sadness hung over everything. I tried to pretend it was okay. So did Jackie. She had a brief affair with Jimmy, but I think it was just to feel close to Rick. After all, he was Rick's friend, and he was a junkie. There were these similarities and, of course, there was always the jazz.

Something tough and hostile was boiling inside of me. I had a slight infatuation with Paulie, but when he returned the sentiments I got scared and didn't really know how to respond. I tried to act like I was experienced, but I was really lost. Paulie was arrested for drug possession, so I never had to expose my innocence to him. I told him I would write to him, pretending to be like Jackie and Rick, but I never wrote a single letter.

I had just turned 17 when a boy that I had liked for three years started to call me. He was a friend of my older brother's. His name was Doug and he looked like James Dean. He was intelligent and exposed me to books, chess and his intellectual friends. I liked him. He showed me a part of life I had never experienced. He thought I was sweet, but he didn't like the way I tried to act hip. He just wanted me to be me. I wasn't sure what that meant. He didn't like Jackie. Just like my parents, he thought she was a bad influence. Sadly enough, I believed him. Or maybe I wanted to believe him, so that I could find my own identity away from the pull of Jackie's life.

My blood ran as cold as the Chicago winter the day I told Jackie that I didn't want to be her friend anymore. "Doug thinks you're a bad influence on me, and so do I." It really didn't matter what I said after that. I had desperately hurt her, and from that moment on, she wouldn't speak to me.

That summer my mother told me that Jackie had received a letter from Frank asking for a divorce. He also wrote that he wanted full custody of Joey. He wasn't angry. He had met someone and felt it was time to move on.

It was a hot summer porch day as I watched from my front room window as Jackie walked out of the courtyard with a suitcase in each hand. She was moving to New York to try to save whatever was left of her marriage. She was ready to fight for her life, and the only future she could see was with Frank. She didn't know I was watching. She didn't know I was crying. She was leaving, and my heart was heavy as I whispered, "Goodbye, Jackie. I love you."

It was 1966. I was 20 years old and singing in nightclubs with a Brazilian jazz group in Los Angeles. Even though I had a job and new friends, I still found myself drawn to my past. I thought about Jackie a lot. Maybe it was guilt, but whatever it was haunted me, and I knew I had to do something about it. It was late when I called New York City information. Her number was listed. My guts were twisting when I heard her sleepy voice.

I was shaking. "Hello, Jackie?"

"Yeah, who's this?" she said.

At first she was cold. I told her I'd been influenced by Doug when I said those awful things. I begged her to forgive me. I told her how important she was to me and how much I loved her and that I would do anything to have her friendship again. She asked me about my life, and kept saying how much I had hurt her. All I could say was how sorry I was, as deep sobs began to surface from the closed door in my heart that was cracking open for the first time in years. I said I would be coming to New York on tour. Sweat was dripping off of me when I hung up the phone. She wanted to see me.

Being with Jackie on that first trip to New York was like a dream. Joey was almost a teenager, and Jackie and Frank had a baby girl now who had the flu. Frank was unchanged, lean and handsome. They looked happier than they had looked in Chicago, but it was hard to tell since they were both so happy to see me.

I took Joey out and bought stamps for his collection, and then I bought presents for everyone. I felt so thankful that my friend had wanted me back in her life. At their apartment we laughed and carried on. She made her great spaghetti to celebrate my visit. They said that they thought I was smart and lovely, and it made me feel grown up. I felt like I was home. Jackie put on "Judy Garland at Carnegie Hall," and I sang "The Man That Got Away" just to see the thrill in her eyes. She cried. That was the closest we came to the past during that first reunion.

It wasn't until the third time I saw Jackie that I wanted to know the answers to some questions that still haunted me. I knew that Frank was out of town and the kids in school. I would be alone with her. In the cab on the way over, I wondered if it would be too painful to bring up buried memories. When I arrived we hugged and laughed. My anxiety grew as the hours passed. Finally, I asked her if she ever thought about Rick.

"Rick who?" she said.

Her response surprised me and she noticed.

"You mean the junkie?" she asked.

I questioned if she still had the love letters they had written to each other when he was in jail. She dropped her eyes when she answered. "I threw everything away when I left Chicago," she said abruptly. "I wanted my new life here with Frank more than anything."

I took a deep breath and asked the question that had been preying on my mind for so long. "Jackie, what do you think would have happened if Rick had lived?"

"Are you kidding?" she said. "He was a junkie! I mean he was nice, but it was nothing. I had no future with him. I would have left him if he hadn't died. Rick and I were an unfortunate fling. That's all."

A freezing chill shot through me. She must have seen the shock on my face. I wanted to be cool, but this was more than I could hide. I swallowed hard before I asked, "But, Jackie, didn't you love him?"

She turned to me with her dark, penetrating eyes and slowly said, "No. I didn't love him." Then she changed the subject.

A little while later I left in a cab similar to the one I had arrived in, only this time I felt like a different passenger. In a daze I watched the brownstones and winter clouds passing by. The driver turned on the radio and asked me what kind of music I liked. "Oh, I like all kinds of music," I answered. Then, almost under my breath, I heard myself say, "But I really like... jazz."

• • •

Epilogue:

Twenty-one years after Rick died, I wrote this story. Frank had died four years earlier in an automobile accident, and Joey was a grown man and on his own. Their daughter was still living at home with Jackie. When I finished writing I picked up the phone and called her.

"Do you have a minute?" I asked.

"Yeah," she said.

I read through the whole story and then waited for her reaction. She was silent for a long time. After she composed herself she spoke with a fragile voice.

"It's not true."

"What's not true?"

"I think about Rick every single day. When you asked me then, I just wanted to rebuild my life with Frank and not think of anything else. But I've thought about Rick every day since he died. I loved him. He was the only man I ever loved."

The light changed from season to season. I was at the mercy of this light. It lifted or plunged me. Tossed me around at will. In winter the street lamps stayed on constantly, and the dark, cold sky competed with the even colder air. The slush of half-melted, dirty snow piled up against the curbs, while cars carefully followed the ghost tracks of traffic on the slow-motion avenues.

The morning sky was never bright enough, and all day long car headlights and street lamps blurred through stinging, teary eyes, assaulted by the wind. The intensity didn't change much from day to night. It was hard to wake up in that darkness. Especially after years of restless sleep.

Nightmares have plagued me all my life. People chasing me, trying to kill me, after me. In other dreams I'll be singing and forget the lyrics, or I'm running and not moving, or falling falling falling. Night visions startle me awake. Spiders descending from the ceiling, people standing near my bed, groups of invaders gathering outside. I've been told I speak a Russian-sounding language when I'm asleep.

I talk and shout out. Or jump out of bed and run away, screaming as I go, brushing imaginary spiders from my hair. My heart pounds so hard I think it will stop or explode. My dreams are so exhausting that my whole day can be lost to fatigue. My mood is dampened. I am in a fog. These visions upset and disturb me.

But other times I am flying over mountains and valleys, the green velvet ground under me as I catch the wind and then land gently on my toes. Those are my favorite dreams, and I am left with a feeling of comfort. Relaxed and hopeful.

I was in therapy for most of my teenage and adult life in search of myself. To find peace. I saw one therapist for 10 years. I would do anything that therapist said, because I didn't trust myself enough to make healthy decisions. It was a dark period in my life. I lost my way for 10 years.

STANDING APPOINTMENT

Five women sat in a small French restaurant chatting quietly, as remnants of the late-afternoon sun gently touched the delicate lace curtains that hung from the dark-paned window. Laura wasn't really listening, she was just watching, occasionally nodding her head in agreement. Her attention suddenly shifted to her best friend, Susan, who was sitting at the far corner of the table. Susan's unblinking eyes were glassy, and she was pointing to her neck, which was an odd, reddish color. Laura was concerned by this quick change of mood, remembering that just two days ago Susan had suffered from a bout of food poisoning. She eased Susan up from her chair to go outside for some fresh air, and they walked through the restaurant, passing the echoes and mumbles of conversation.

Once outside, they went down a flight of stone steps, stopping at a landing with a small sitting area where Susan immediately put her head in a garbage can. Laura pulled up each side of her full skirt to shield Susan from this embarrassment. The sunset breeze blew the silky fabric like a flag.

When Susan finished throwing up, she told Laura to go back to the restaurant. She was feeling self-conscious, afraid that Laura was attracting too much attention by lifting her skirt. Laura agreed to go, but as she looked back she saw Susan running away. It seemed that some people who worked at the restaurant were angry that she had been ill so close by.

Walking back to the restaurant, Laura wondered how long she had kept the other women waiting. It was starting to get dark and it seemed as if it were taking much longer to get back. People on the other side of the street were watching her. Some of them were the ones that had been yelling at Susan. Laura wondered why they had been so insensitive and had made such a fuss. Maybe it was their fancy French food that had made Susan sick.

Up ahead, in the middle of the sidewalk, a workman had left two rather high piles of sand with deep pits on either side. Laura didn't want to walk across the street to avoid the sand piles because the angry people were just starting to disperse, so she casually stepped into the loose sand and began to climb. The sand was damp and stuck to her legs as she moved through it. When she reached the top of the pile, she turned and saw the deep pit behind her. She didn't really think she would fall, but as she moved she lost her footing and fell backwards into the pit.

It was much deeper than it looked, and the soft, damp sand on the bottom was also deep. It was pulling her under fast. She started to yell for help but sand got in her mouth. She was going under. She was going to die and no one would ever find her body. Susan would call her apartment later, while the other women would wait at the restaurant. After a time they would probably contact each other, not knowing what had happened, and Laura's cold body would be breathlessly lost under the sand.

Laura clawed at the air, jerking up from under the covers. Her heart was racing as she gasped. She walked into the bathroom to splash cold water on her face. When she saw her pale reflection in the mirror, she whispered, "God, I hate this."

"I hate this, Dr. Portugese! Why do I have these awful dreams? They stay with me all day. It's so upsetting, and if you're not available, what am I supposed to do?" Laura's thin legs were crossed and her top foot was drawing invisible patterns in the air. She was troubled by these frightening dreams, and when she looked up and saw the expression on her psychologist's face, she knew that all the wrinkles on her forehead were showing.

Dr. Portugese had often said that by the time she reached 40, which wouldn't be for another eight years, her forehead would look like a road map if she didn't stop scrunching it up. She waited impatiently for his answer.

"Okay, Laura, let's figure this one out. You've got Susan and some new women in a lovely French restaurant, and you notice the details. Susan gets sick. You go down steps – down steps." He looked up at her. "Going down staircases always means creativity to you, Laura." He continued, "And who's Susan? Your best friend... your confidante... your wisdom, I think. And these new women. Very positive. *New* adventure. *New* things. Okay. Susan gets sick. You leave. But, Laura, look here! You notice so many details. Appreciating everything. *Very* positive. Susan runs away, leaving you on your own. Good! You're independently going back to your new experience, and what happens? You ignore the people who are watching you, and you stand your ground. 'Maybe it's the restaurant food,' you say. No self-doubt. No self-blame. This is a *very* positive dream, Laura."

"But what about the sand, Dr. Portugese?" she moaned. "I die in this dream!"

He replied, a bit irritated, "You want to get hysterical? I'm telling you that so far it's a very positive dream, and you're sinking with the negatives."

"Yes, but..." she uttered.

He interrupted, "I don't want to hear it! Don't use up the air on negativity."

He took a deep breath and continued, "The sand is conflict. That's all it represents. You confront the conflict, which is deciding to climb the sand pile, and it swallows you up. It just shows that you don't have the inner confidence to confront this new experience yet. That's all it is. But if you want to make it the event of the week…"

"No! No, I don't," she cried.

When he spoke he seemed to look through her. "Laura, when you started coming here five years ago, you were, I would say, a borderline psychotic. You had phobias, you looked terrible and you weren't doing anything with your life. You were a real flake. Now look at you. Your art career is taking off and you look terrific. When you start to think negative thoughts, look around and find something pretty. Put your attention there. You were all upset about this dream, and I view it as very positive. Doesn't that tell you something about the way you interpret things?"

Laura trusted Dr. Portugese more than she trusted herself. "Yes," she replied. "It tells me how much I need you."

He stood up. "If you want to beat yourself up, go ahead. It's hard for anyone to see themselves objectively. I'll see you next Thursday."

As always, before leaving, she asked the same question. "So how do you think I'm doing?"

As always, he responded with the same answer. "How do *you* think you're doing?"

On the way to her car she thought to herself, "I'm together. Probably more together than most people. I just have to remember to look for the positives." But a hidden doubt, that she skillfully covered, gnawed at her, and occasionally she would hear its muffled cry.

The figures in front of her began to dissolve. She found herself sitting on her living room floor in her pajamas, talking to a group of imaginary people. It was almost four in the morning and she was now fully awake. She didn't know how long she had been sitting there. It was the sound of her own voice that had finally awakened her. Laura started laughing as she pulled herself up, but there was a strange shakiness inside her body that she ignored.

Lately, her dreams were becoming so vivid that by morning she would be too exhausted to get up and would sleep past noon. When her friends asked what she had been doing, she would usually lie, guilt-ridden about not having accomplished what she thought was expected of her. She never told Dr. Portugese about these "lazy days," as she called them.

Laura was a passionate artist. Her paintings had a unique, sweeping, musical quality that were, like her, unpredictable. Since she started seeing Dr. Portugese, she had hired an agent and now produced much more art. A hot new gallery was showing some of her work and wanted to set a date for a one-woman show.

She used to try to schedule and organize her days so that she would be as productive and efficient as possible. If she felt a little under the weather, Dr. Portugese would tell her to ignore it, and that's exactly what she did. She did everything Dr. Portugese told her to do. She felt that he knew the healthiest way for her to live her life, even though her friends would tell her that her dependency on him seemed unhealthy.

She hadn't been spending any time with her friends or family lately, and it worried her. There was a growing unrest in her that most people dismissed as artist's temperament, and that Dr. Portugese wanted her to ignore.

All day there were power failures in the neighborhood where Laura rented an art studio. The electric company had been working under the street for weeks, adding cables and infuriating shop owners and residents. Her airbrush would shut off at crucial moments, and she temporarily changed her style to accommodate the electrical problems.

It was getting late and the light had already left the evening sky. Before going home, she decided to take a walk in the looming darkness. The area was normally very busy, but now, because of the power shortages, the streets were empty and she felt invisible passing familiar shops and cafes.

She looked in the window of a bakery on the corner, and in the dim light it seemed to transform into a French country inn. She imagined being in a small village in France, renting a single room with a fireplace and spending the rest of her life there. When reality seeped back into her consciousness, her fantasy evaporated and she went home and crawled into bed.

Laura's eyes snapped open and focused on the silhouette of a large man standing in the shadows near her. Frozen with fear, she struggled to keep her mind clear. Jumping out of bed, she raced to the kitchen and grabbed her largest knife and smashed her hand on the burglar alarm setting it ringing throughout her apartment. All at once the thought occurred to her that she might have imagined the whole thing. She cautiously went to the bedroom. No one was there. She sat on the bed and called the patrol to cancel the false alarm. The rest of the night she stared at the ceiling, too afraid to go back to sleep.

Dr. Portugese spoke with authority and power. "Laura, you are a highly intelligent, very talented and creative woman. You also have a great imagination. That's why you're an artist, for God's sake! Imagination and creativity go hand in hand. I've seen a lot of people in my 20-year practice, and you are unique. You have a rich character and a lot of substance, but you have a very short memory for your own accomplishments."

She knew that he must be breathing between sentences, but she couldn't see him take in any air. He continued. "You have no real problems, Laura, just things that need tending. I want you to say that to yourself when you start to worry. Whenever negatives pop into your mind, I want you to tell yourself that you have no real problems. Then change the picture, look for something positive and get to work. I don't think you're busy enough. That's why your negative imagination is taking over. Your subconscious is bored, and, to tell you the truth, you're starting to bore me too." He raised his voice and pointed his finger at her. "Move your ass more and you won't have time to worry. Then when you go to sleep, you'll be tired enough to rest everything, including your subconscious."

Laura stared at Dr. Portugese. She wondered why she couldn't do it right. "Do you think I'm crazy?" she asked.

He answered abruptly, "Don't you think *I* would know if you were crazy? I've had years of experience working in mental institutions. I do admit when you first came to me you were borderline, but now you don't come close to being crazy."

He swiveled his chair and turned his back to her as he continued speaking. "You think too much. *Do* more and you won't have time to think about being crazy."

"But is it normal to have these kinds of experiences?" she asked.

He faced her and responded impatiently. "It isn't abnormal to wake up and think you see objects or people in the room with you. It's a kind of limbo consciousness, the state between dreaming and waking. You're just seeing trails of your dreams. That's all. Don't bother making it more than it is. The images you're seeing simply have to do with your creative imagination."

Dr. Portugese signaled the end of the session by looking at his watch. His abrupt tone frightened Laura out of asking any more questions. She didn't want him to be mad at her, and she left his office feeling unsettled. She desperately wanted his words to ease her anxiety, and was sure he was right about everything he said. She didn't want to feel so afraid, and took his advice by changing the picture. She looked up at the passing clouds, but all that she saw in the cloud formations were strange, gliding monsters that frightened her even more.

Dr. Portugese sat in his living room looking at his wife, who was passed out on the sofa, dead drunk. The loving family photographs around their house and his office were a complete masquerade. He knew from the moment he married her that it was a mistake. She came from a wealthy family and promised to put him through school, and she never let him forget that without her support and connections he would have never made it.

She disgusted him, begging him to touch her, holding the money over his head every time he wanted to leave her. And when that didn't work she would threaten to ruin him. Expose his deepest secrets. Slander his reputation as a respectable psychotherapist. At times he would hit her, but she seemed to want that kind of abusive attention. She knew it excited him, and would laugh at his weakness, pick herself off the floor, peel off her clothes and force him between her legs. It always ended with her lying on the bed, threatening him until he satisfied her.

This evening he had to escape. He drove to a department store in his neighborhood that was open at night. He breezed through several floors until something on a far wall caught his eye. It was a hand-carved wooden pipe perched on a Lucite stand. The design was abstract, and he couldn't figure out what it was supposed to be, but he didn't care. He liked its ambiguity.

He stood in front of it, pretending to be looking at the other items on the shelves. With his head turned to the right, he carefully took hold of the pipe and casually put it in his pocket. Just as he was about to leave, a male voice interrupted him.

"It really is unusual, isn't it?" Dr. Portugese turned around and faced the salesman, who was pointing at a lava lamp not five inches from his face. He looked at the blue slime that pretended to be the ocean, rolling around in a clear, plastic cylinder. He didn't respond and walked away, sweating slightly through his neatly pressed shirt.

When he arrived home he went directly to his den and, with the only key, he unlocked a solid mahogany cabinet. Displayed inside was a vast assortment of modern and antique cigarette cases and lighters with price tags dangling from each one. His need for a pipe was just about as useless as his need for anything inside the cabinet. Dr. Portugese didn't smoke.

It was a bright Sunday afternoon. Laura decided to meet some friends at the aquarium and then go with them for an early dinner. Some of the small exhibits on the main floor were blacked out, making Laura wonder what lurked behind. One of her friends put her arm around Laura's waist, guiding her into the elevator. Before entering,

Laura noticed a sign stating the third floor was closed for remodeling. At the first stop, Laura stepped out. Realizing her error, she turned back, but the elevator had moved on, and now she stood alone on the third floor.

The entire space was the size of a large ballroom. The floor, ceiling and all four walls were thick plate glass, with aquamarine water behind. It was a strange, suspended feeling to be totally surrounded by water. Laura walked to the center of the room. She knew that if she waited long enough, surely her friends would come back for her.

She looked down into the blue water. She saw something moving in the distance, and as it came closer she focused until she could identify it. A giant octopus was propelling toward her with its outreached tentacles, spewing clouds of black ink as it moved closer. When her head jerked up, giant manta rays flew by with their huge, gaping mouths hanging open, while hammerhead sharks stalked from behind. Everywhere she turned was another silent creature circling around her.

Suddenly, everything scattered. A great white shark cut through the water at high speed, slamming against the glass. She backed away from rows of razor sharp teeth, and the only sound she could hear was the pounding of the shark's snout against the cracking glass. Sparkling beads of water dripped at Laura's feet until the thick glass could no longer hold back the savage power. Laura began to shake uncontrollably as it crashed through the glass, its hungry mouth, wide open, ready to devour her.

Over the next few weeks Laura didn't go to her art studio. She had no appetite and would sleep until the late afternoon. She didn't mention this to Dr. Portugese, and even cancelled some appointments because she knew it would disappoint him. She felt like a failure. A weakling. A bad patient. She turned off her answering machine and didn't see anyone.

After another day of waking up late she opened her refrigerator and saw a fuzzy, green mold covering the food inside. A living substance, growing in clusters, had also attached itself to the side walls. She pulled up a chair and sat in front of the open refrigerator for hours. She wanted to see the infectious spores multiply. Maybe they would take over her kitchen, her apartment. Her life.

She wondered if she kept the refrigerator door open when she went to sleep, would she wake up covered in the sticky, moss-like organism, like a layer of long green hair that she could wear instead of clothing? That would grow and feed on her body until there was nothing left but a carpet of green, like the everglades or an ancient rain forest, where she could hide until it was safe to come back.

In the middle of the night, again and again, she found her nightgown soaked through, and as soon as she wiped the perspiration from her forehead it came right back. But she wasn't hot. She was freezing cold, and it wasn't from the lack of heat in the room. It came from her deepest, most hidden core. And when she fell back to sleep, she left her leg dangling off the edge of the bed, ready to run.

It wasn't the ringing telephone that awakened her. It was the crack of sunlight coming through a small opening in the drapes that caught her eye. She hadn't answered the phone in weeks, but this time she picked it up before she could think not to.

The woman on the other end screamed, "Laura? Is that you?"

"Yes," she answered, her brain still foggy.

"Thank God! I've been trying to get you for weeks! Anyway, I've got you now. It's the gallery calling. What's happening with the new paintings you promised me?" If the sunlight and the ringing phone didn't fully awaken her, this woman's piercing voice most certainly did.

"Well, they're not exactly ready yet," Laura answered.

The woman screeched, "Not ready yet? We've sold all but one of your paintings! People want to see your work, Laura! They ask daily! One hotel owner is even thinking of commissioning you to do his new lobby, and if he likes it, he'll hire you to do the entire hotel! I don't think you understand what kind of momentum we have going here. I have a big check for you, and I'll only give it to you if you come down here in person. How about noon?" Laura felt lighter. The day was bright and this conversation made her feel better.

The woman at the gallery jumped up when Laura entered and asked if she'd like to join her for lunch. Laura didn't want this meeting to be any longer than necessary and she declined, even though she hadn't eaten in days and her stomach was gurgling from emptiness. The woman not only spoke of clients and interviews but also of a TV special of upcoming local artists, and an all expenses paid trip to New York, where there was a genuine interest in Laura's work.

When the woman gave her the envelope, Laura didn't open it until she got in her car, where she stared at the check for at least 20 minutes. She had always been insecure about her work, but this was a confirmation that she had the talent to communicate. Motivated and inspired to work, she went to her studio and painted all day and well into the night. Her exhaustion finally stopped her, and the last thing she saw before she dozed off was the twilight glow of dawn dissolving the night sky.

Laura was in her childhood apartment with her mother and father. She noticed green smoke coming from under the front door. Her parents ran out the back door, but instead of following them, Laura ran to their bedroom and locked the door.

Panic-stricken, she wondered if she should have gone with her parents, but it was too late to change her mind. She heard low groans and demonic rumbles coming from outside the bedroom door. Laura took a deep breath and flung the door wide open, coming face to face with a devil. His ugliness was unbearable, and she felt his hot breath on her skin. She wanted to run, but she didn't. She matched his stare, and when she had the courage to speak, she looked into his blood-red eyes and said with conviction, "Sometimes you must face head on what you are most afraid of." Suddenly, the devil looked frightened, turned back to green smoke and disappeared.

A few hours later, Laura woke up feeling an inner peace. She lay in bed watching shadows mixing with sprinkled light that played on the ceiling while she reflected on her dream. Genuinely excited, she lifted herself out of bed. It was 8:30 a.m. She raced to get dressed. She didn't want to be late for her 9:15 standing appointment with Dr. Portugese.

He was writing at his desk when his secretary buzzed his office that Laura had arrived. Laura greeted him cheerfully, but he didn't raise his head to look at her when he answered. "Just one minute, I have to finish this note."

His face appeared somber. Her eyes drifted over his body and she noticed that he wasn't wearing the wedding ring she had always admired, and some of the family pictures were missing from his desk and bookshelves. On occasion, she had wondered about his personal life, but she had never asked him. Until today.

"How's your family, Dr. Portugese?"

He looked up at her. His face was very still. "You know, Laura," he said slowly, "this is the first time you've ever asked me about my family. Tell me, what pulled you out of your self-obsessed world long enough to notice that there are people who are doing things in their lives that have nothing to do with you?"

She was stunned by his response. "I was just curious, that's all."

"Curious?" he said. "Well, that's very interesting. I guess curious is better than boring."

He walked to the window and looked out at the brown cloud hovering over the city, mumbling under his breath, "If my wife doesn't kill me, this smog probably will."

Laura interrupted, "What's wrong, Dr. Portugese?"

He snapped back, "We're here to talk about you. This is your appointment, remember?"

Laura felt a growing tightness in her stomach. Wanting to change the mood, she said, "I'm feeling better today."

"Oh, I'm so glad, because I don't think I could take another one of your depression sessions today. I mean, Laura, are you aware that there are a lot of women who would want very much to live your life? You have talent and a career, but you continue to come here every week, sounding like a bottomless pit that keeps screaming, 'fill me, fill me!'"

His voice was piercing. Laura was having trouble keeping eye contact with him and began to fidget with her hands. She sensed that the room was slowly revolving.

His tone was filled with sarcasm, "But I'm so glad you're feeling better." Then he abruptly asked, "Any interesting dreams?"

When she focused on her latest dream she felt a momentary lift in the strange atmosphere that permeated his office. She said, "Yes, I had a dream that I really feel good about."

He put his glasses on and wrote as Laura told him every detail of her dream. When she finished she watched him with anticipation, wondering if he thought her dream was as positive as she felt it was.

He sat quietly contemplating the written words. Finally, he broke the silence. "This dream clearly shows that you see yourself as a horrible, ugly, evil creature."

Laura's head felt heavy. From the corner of her eye she thought she saw a woman in a long black dress, sitting on the edge of the sofa reading a book, but when she looked no one was there. Meanwhile, Dr. Portugese continued his analysis. "In this dream your parents abandon you and the green smoke sliding under the door most definitely means that you feel you're slime. After all, you're everything and everyone in the dream."

"But Dr. Portugese…"

He interrupted her, but failed to look in her eyes as he spoke. "Laura, I've been meaning to talk to you, and now is as good a time as any. I'm going to make some changes. I'm thinking of writing a book, and well, anyway, I don't feel I have anything left to give to you—emotionally speaking that is, and, uh, I'm sorry to say that I'm terminating your therapy. I have referrals if you need someone, but today will be our last appointment."

The clouds passing in front of the sun cast strange, moving shadows on the wall. Laura's eyes darted back and forth. She didn't hear his words anymore. She was lost in a fog of panic, and she desperately wanted to get away from herself. Jumping up, she cried, "Dr. Portugese! I forgot to tell you. I have a surprise for you!"

He jerked his head up, "What? What is it?"

"Close your eyes! If you close your eyes you'll get a big surprise!" she shouted.

For a brief moment he wondered if she had bought him a pipe for his office display collection. A slight smile crossed his face as he closed his eyes. In one motion Laura picked up a silver letter opener from his desk and with all her might pushed it deeply into his left eye. She did it with such force that just before the metal sliced through his brain, his eye popped out of its socket and onto his desk. She watched the trickle of blood seeping from the wound. It reminded her of the trickling water from the crack in the aquarium glass, and she couldn't remember if that had been a dream or if it had really happened.

Dr. Portugese sat perfectly still. Then, she saw his ocean blue eye settled on his desk. The fleshy globe watched her as she walked over to the window to sit on the sill. She looked out at the city but didn't feel connected to the view.

The intercom was buzzing, but Laura continued to stare out the window. His secretary knocked quietly and then peeked in to tell Dr. Portugese that his wife was on the phone. She stood in the doorway wearing a short skirt. Laura turned to her and said, "You have the prettiest legs I've ever seen. Are they yours?" The secretary looked confused, and when she saw Dr. Portugese slumped in the chair she gasped and ran out.

Time had stopped. Clouds were moving in the sky, and people were walking outside, but the room was completely still. Even with all the commotion coming from the outer office, Laura continued to stare out the window. She was waiting to wake up. She hoped she would remember this dream so that she could tell it to Dr. Portugese. He would think this one was very interesting.

Emotional Memoirs

In winter, people huddled inside the tiny train station on my corner to avoid the bitter cold on the outside platform. The floor of the station was puddled with slush from the galoshes of people buying tokens and transfers, or from going to the tiny newsstand in the corner that was bathed in golden, incandescent light.

The little man that stood in the narrow space behind the newsstand wore a cap, and a cigar poked out from the side of his mouth. His short, stubby fingers and broken fingernails were permanently ink-stained from years of selling newspapers and magazines. His eyes never looked up at the faces of his customers. They saw only print and change, watching hands and racks of paper.

We were the last stop. The end of the Ravenswood line on Kimball and Lawrence Avenues. It looks like a bus terminal now. The old station was torn down decades ago, but I can still see it so clearly in my mind. Going through the turnstile to buy a ticket from the lady in the dim light behind the barred stall, I'd pass by the newsstand and prepare myself for the indescribable cold blast that led outside. The lights flickered on and off from inside the trains as they pulled in and out, while the screeching sound of metal on metal stung my ears.

I was 18 years old then, and had joined the work force as a file clerk at Who's Who in America on Chicago's Near North side. I'd change trains at Belmont station to take the subway, and when I walked up from the tunnels of the city I'd pass the stately brownstones and expensive stores that lined Michigan Avenue. I curled around Oak Street, entered the building and daydreamed my way through the boredom of that job.

But there was a romance about the "el" trains and the young men, fresh out of college, starting their careers, standing on the platforms in their business suits. Belmont station was the highlight of my day. Every morning I'd wait for the train and for Mr. Belmont. That's what I called him. He would be sitting on the platform bench reading the newspaper, with his attaché case placed beside his freshly shined shoes. We never talked, although he did say, "Hello" to me once. That's all. But that one "Hello" carried me for months.

MR. BELMONT

His blond hair glistened in the early spring sun. The sound of the approaching train startled Sarah out of her daydream. She stepped onto the train looking for an empty double seat, hoping, as she did every morning, that he would sit next to her. Just as she slid by the window, a rather plump, older woman sat down beside her. Mr. Belmont was left standing, holding the bar above. Sarah watched his eyes as they followed the outside images.

She named him Mr. Belmont because every morning at 8:40 she changed trains at Belmont Station, and every morning she saw him. When her stop came up, she decided that this morning she would continue on to see where he got off. A daring move for a married woman.

The train collected more people as it moved from station to station. Suddenly, his hand disappeared from the bar and he stepped off at Merchandise Mart. Sarah jumped up to follow him, crushing her knees against the fat woman, but halfway to the door the entire contents of her purse spilled to the floor. As the doors closed, the last image she saw of him was the blur of his blue three-piece suit.

"What's up?" Karen said, standing in the doorway, out of breath. "You sounded so frantic on the phone."

Sarah stared at Karen's pale face before she whispered, "I think I'm in love, and I don't mean with Michael."

Karen's disbelieving voice broke through the silence. "Don't do this to me, Sarah. You have the perfect marriage. Who are you talking about?"

"He's a guy I see on the 'el' every morning. He's tall, thin and blond. Blond, Karen. You know I never even notice blondes. He always wears a three-piece suit and carries a brown attaché case. He's very quiet and serious, and the other day he said hello to me... I think."

Karen questioned her slowly. "You mean you've never *actually* spoken to him?" Her tone changed from confused to abrupt. "I don't get it. All my life I've wanted what you have. You married Prince Charming. You have a successful editing career. What else do you want?"

Sadness tinged Sarah's voice. "I never told you this, but I hardly ever see Michael anymore. By the time I wake up he's leaving for work, and when he comes home I'm usually asleep. He's always talking about finding the meaning of life and... it just feels like I'm not that important to him anymore."

Karen put her arm around Sarah's shoulder and urged her, "Tell him what you're feeling, Sarah. He'll understand. He loves you. He'd want to know."

Sarah turned away, "Don't you think I've tried? He's so introspective he can't even hear me. We're just not on the same track anymore, and I can't stop thinking about Mr. Belmont." She faced Karen. "This is more than a crush, Karen. I know what I'm feeling, and I think I'm falling in love with him."

Sarah's sleepy eyes stared at the sun's patterns scattered on the bedroom ceiling, but when Michael came into the room she immediately pretended to be asleep. "Sarah, it's 6:15! Come on, get up!" he called. She stretched her slim body to its limits, sending a rush of blood to her head that made her dizzy. As Michael left the room he called out, "Oh yeah, I almost forgot. I'm working late, so I won't be home for dinner."

She let her nightgown fall to the bathroom floor and stepped into a steamy shower. Michael's piercing voice yelled "Sarah! It's 6:45!" His head was in the shower and tiny beads of water fell onto his dark hair, giving it a gray cast, making him look much older than his 35 years. Sarah unconsciously covered her breasts with her hands. "What are you doing?" he asked. His puzzled look made her feel foolish. She didn't know why she had covered herself. She dropped her hands and said, "Have a nice day." He closed the shower door and yelled, "You too." She knew that was the last she would see of Michael until the next morning.

Their relationship troubled her more each day. Though they rarely argued, in recent months she felt a silent indifference growing between them. He phoned less during the day, and his calls were hurried. There was a time when Michael had shown an interest in every aspect of her life. Their long talks in bed had been some of the most intimate moments she had ever experienced. She missed those talks even more than she missed his passion for her. Sometimes when she looked at him now, she sensed that she was doomed to live a loveless life that simply passed from day to day.

His long legs moved like slow music. She got off the train at Merchandise Mart, and walked several feet behind him, intensely aware of her silk slip clinging to her body from the humidity. She followed him and, just as she stepped into the lobby from the revolving door, she caught a glimpse of him buying the morning paper before getting in the elevator. The building directory showed that most of the people working there were either in commodities or law. Mr. Belmont, she thought, was definitely a lawyer.

Sarah left work early to wait for him at Merchandise Mart. It was six o'clock, and everyone was rushing to leave. When she spotted him, he looked more relaxed than he had in the morning. His tie was loosened and his blond hair fell, ever so slightly, onto his forehead. He was standing by the elevators talking casually to a small group. A smile danced on his face, brightening it, adding an iridescent glow to his blue-green eyes. Yet, what dazzled her most were his dimples, one planted on each cheek that deepened when he laughed. They added a gentle charm to his masculinity.

He left the building with three men. Instead of walking toward the train station, they crossed a busy intersection that led them under the rush-hour howl of the train tracks, into a bar called The Mart. Red and white neon lights flashed every now and then, and sawdust covered the floor. A semicircular, mahogany bar was in the center of the crowded room, and she found Mr. Belmont standing at the end, talking to his three friends.

She squeezed in behind them, ordered a drink and stood motionless, her profile etched in air. While her fingers cleared the cold mist on her glass one of his friends reached for a bowl of nuts, accidentally spilling her white wine on her dress. The very next moment Sarah felt a hand touching her right shoulder. Mr. Belmont was looking directly into her eyes, not 10 inches from her face. "Are you all right?" he asked.

She breathed deeply. "Yes, I-I'm fine, it's only white wine." Her stomach churned. "Thank you for asking." He smiled warmly and turned away. His voice was deeper and quieter than she had imagined. She was trembling.

He turned back to her. "Excuse me, but if I don't ask you this question it'll be on my mind all night. Have we met before?" he asked.

She watched his inquiring gaze and thought, "Well Sarah, you've finagled your way into meeting him. Now what?" She replied softly, "I don't think so."

"Do you work around here?" he asked.

"No, I work as an editor at Who's Who in America around Michigan and Oak. Do you work around there?"

"No. I work at a law firm at Merchandise Mart," he answered. "But you look so familiar."

She smiled and said, "Well, that happens sometimes."

Just as she was about to introduce herself, one of his friends shouted, "Hey, David, come on, we'll miss the train!"

Mr. Belmont's smile faded. "Well, goodbye stranger," he said, before disappearing into the crowd. She couldn't move. She just sat there, quietly repeating over and over to herself, "His name is David."

She imagined what it would be like to be single again and live in a small apartment by the lake. She envisioned paned windows that looked out, like eyeglasses, onto the water view and stark white walls for her Van Gogh and Renoir prints. She would play her favorite music, any time she wanted to, in her private sanctuary.

Michael never listened to music. Even before they were married she noticed the silence. In the beginning she'd listen by herself, but after a while she packed all of her CDs and stacked them on a shelf in the hall closet.

Only a year before, Michael and Sarah had been filled with a tender passion for each other, but slowly Michael began to change. He became preoccupied with finding his life's purpose. He attacked new projects at work with an aggression that pushed Sarah, and everything else, away. He no longer wanted to discuss having a baby. He said that he couldn't raise a child until he knew what he wanted from life. There were still some sweet moments between them, but most of the time a heavy, alienating cloud hung over him.

The more she tried to talk to him about their relationship, the more he retreated into his work. When he refused to see a marriage counselor, communication between them stopped. Unable to think of any other way of reaching Michael, and not wanting to make a hasty decision, her lonely heart closed to him.

Now, her fantasies were all that satisfied her. When they would occasionally make love, Sarah imagined being wrapped inside Mr. Belmont's embrace. Afterward, while Michael slept, she'd take her pillow into the den and sink into the down-filled couch. The street lamp glow from outside would fill the room with candlelit softness as her hands moved over her arched body as she surrendered herself to her dream of Mr. Belmont.

The spring sun was strong, and even though his eyes were hidden behind his dark glasses she knew that he was watching her. She looked away self-consciously and saw the approaching train in the distance. When she turned back toward him her knees weakened. He was standing in front of her. "Hello, stranger! Remember me?" he asked. "From the bar near Merchandise Mart. My friend spilled your drink. White wine, right?"

She was looking at her shaky reflection in his sunglasses. "Oh yes, I remember," she eked out.

His large, warm hand swallowed her smallness. "I'm David Mitchell," he said. As they talked, the current of the crowd moved them onto the train. She felt intoxicated sitting next to him. She wanted to walk around Grant Park or go to the Lincoln Park Zoo with him. She longed to show him the painting of Van Gogh's room at the Art Institute or just sit on the elevated train to the end of the line. Colors looked brighter, and she could swear that she smelled the distant lilac bushes from inside the train.

"Isn't this your stop?" he asked. As she stood up he smiled at her and said, "Maybe I'll see you again tomorrow."

Sarah watched from the platform, and as the train disappeared it seemed to pull all the color with it, except for her thoughts of Mr. Belmont.

They met every day for the next three weeks at Belmont Station. She seldom talked about her life, wanting to know more about him. He talked about his childhood and his career, and also mentioned that he had recently broken up with a woman he'd been seeing for the past five years, but that they still occasionally saw each other. Only once she revealed that she was married, and that things were getting difficult at home, but she felt uncomfortable and disloyal talking to him about Michael, so she avoided it after that first discussion.

Mr. Belmont played the trumpet on weekends at a jazz club on Rush Street. He said that it was a great release from the pressures of his job and that it gave him a feeling of freedom he couldn't find anywhere else. She said that she would love to hear him play. "Bring your husband," he suggested. She didn't answer.

On Sunday night Sarah called Karen, begging her to go to Rush Street with her to see Mr. Belmont. Karen reluctantly gave in to Sarah's pleadings, but only after repeatedly stating that she thought it was a terrible idea. Sarah dressed carefully, trying to look different from the way Mr. Belmont had seen her each morning. She told Michael that she and Karen were going to a movie and that she'd probably be home late. It was the first time she had ever lied to him.

There was no stage in the smoky bar, and the muted lighting silhouetted the four-piece band in the corner. They took a table in the back, and when Sarah spotted Mr. Belmont he was standing in the shadows, leaning against a wall waiting for the piano player to finish his solo.

His silver horn caught the colored reflections of the dimly lit club. There was an intimacy between Mr. Belmont and the seductive sound that he created with his horn.

She wished that she knew more about jazz and questioned Karen, who had only heard of Miles Davis and who added again that she thought it was a bad idea for them to be there. When the last set was over, Mr. Belmont came over to Sarah's table looking genuinely surprised to see her. "You sound a little like Miles Davis," she said. He seemed flattered and invited them to go for a late night drink at The Mart. Karen declined and, with her eyes, urged Sarah to do the same, but it was a hopeless gesture. Sarah lit up at Mr. Belmont's request, and by the smile on his face it looked as though he was happy with her quick response.

In a cab on the way, Sarah talked about how exciting it was to hear him play. He didn't say much. He simply watched her as if he were being entertained. It made her feel as if he wanted to be with her.

When they arrived, he introduced her to a few of his friends. Suddenly, out of nowhere, a strange wave of anxiety flooded through her. The noise in the room intensified, and she couldn't concentrate because she was thinking about Michael. It was late, and she was worried that he might call Karen's apartment looking for her. She knew that Karen would cover for her, but she still felt like a teenager who was staying out past curfew.

She jumped up, "I've got to go," she said. "It was a great evening. I'll see you tomorrow."

Mr. Belmont looked puzzled. "Is anything wrong?"

She grabbed her purse saying, "Oh, no! I just noticed the time and didn't realize it was so late. I have to go now. Goodnight."

Mr. Belmont stopped her and because of the late hour insisted on taking her home. He hailed a cab and now she was the silent one as they drove to her apartment. While he talked she couldn't stop thinking about Michael. Her skin felt hot against the night air, as if her blood were rushing too quickly through her body.

When she got home, she nervously tiptoed to the bedroom and was relieved to find that Michael was sleeping. Alone in the bathroom she thought about what had just happened. It was almost more than she could bear... her first date with Mr. Belmont.

Mr. Belmont wasn't at the train station. She figured he had probably slept late, so she waited for him on the wooden bench where he usually sat reading the morning paper. Three trains later she wondered if he were sick, or worse yet, avoiding her.

She left work early and went to look for him at his office building but couldn't find him. The only place left for her to try was The Mart. When she walked in she scanned the crowd. He wasn't there. She sat at the bar and wondered if his phone number was listed.

Just as she was about to check she heard his voice behind her. "What are you doing here, Sarah?"

She spun around and was almost overcome with emotion when she saw him. "I'm so glad to see you! I was really worried about you! Are you all right?"

He didn't answer right away. When he finally did, he chose his words carefully. "Sarah, I'm beginning to feel uncomfortable. I think we're getting too close. I mean, I like you and I've enjoyed being with you very much, but something else seems to be starting, and it just doesn't feel right. Do you understand what I'm saying?"

She sensed a profound sadness and tried to change his mind. "But nothing has happened between us. We're just friends. Why should we stop seeing each other?" He looked at her intensely for a moment and then glanced away. She noticed his fingers pulling at his school ring. It made her wonder how many young girls had worn this golden circle on chains around their necks, or had wrapped the back with tape to wear on their delicate fingers. She touched his coat sleeve and broke the silence with a flirtatious whisper. "Don't you know that I find you irresistible?"

A shine came to his eyes and they both started to laugh. He ordered a drink and they stayed at the bar, talking nervously, skillfully avoiding what he had said earlier. A while later they went to a small Italian restaurant around the corner. When she picked up the menu he asked her what she liked. "I like the sound of your voice," she murmured.

When they left the restaurant she curled her arm through his and he didn't say anything. He accepted her actions and words, and that encouraged her even more. He hailed a cab for her, and just before she got in she quickly kissed his lips. As he stood on the curb she closed the taxi door and watched him, watching her, roll away.

When she awoke she opened the bedroom window wide, breathing in the sweetness of spring. The buds on the trees were straining to break open, impatient to show their colors. When Michael came into the room his voice startled her. "Sarah, I have to leave for New York tomorrow. An important contract has come up for the company. I won't be gone that long. I'll be back on Wednesday. It's only five days."

There had been a time when being away from Michael for only five days would have seemed like an eternity. Days would feel like weeks, and when he'd return she'd feel safe and complete again.

She knew that he was watching her reaction carefully. "I think it's fine," she said, unable to meet his eyes. "A lot of people are counting on you and, like you said, it's only five days."

When he left the following morning there was so little emotion between them that she wondered if he were looking forward to his time away from her, but she didn't think about Michael for long. She could only think about the next few days and Mr. Belmont.

That morning, on the train, she casually mentioned that if he were playing on Rush Street that evening she'd like to go and hear him play. Her blood ran cold when he told her that his ex-girlfriend would be there.

That night she took a warm, scented bath and dressed rather seductively. Her dark eyes looked luminous against the blush of her cheeks and she was positive that something was about to happen.

The club was overflowing with people. There were no available tables. Sarah inched her way to the bar and was lucky enough to find an empty stool near the cash register. She looked around, paying careful attention to the women in the club who were alone.

The sound of his trumpet pierced through her. Mr. Belmont closed his eyes as he played. When he finished his solo it took him a while to focus, and when he did he still looked far away. He picked up his drink and just before he sipped it Sarah noticed a slight smile cross his face. She followed his eyes to a table where a blonde woman was watching him. She was actually lovelier than Sarah had imagined. Her hair was silky and straight. She and Mr. Belmont blended with their long, graceful bodies and blondness.

Sarah sat in the shadows, and after the last set she watched the club spill onto the street. It was closing time, and Mr. Belmont approached the bar to pay his tab. When he saw Sarah he stopped cold. "What are you doing here, Sarah? How long have you been sitting at the bar?"

"Long enough," she said.

"Are you alone? It's so late. Won't your husband be worried?"

In a challenging tone, she said, "Michael is out of town until Wednesday."

They watched each other carefully. Sarah knew the blonde woman was listening to the silence between them. She approached them saying, "David, are we going now?" Then, she turned to Sarah. "Hello, I'm Jean Whitman." She extended her hand and Sarah took it, eager to feel the hand that had touched him so intimately.

Mr. Belmont's eyes never left Sarah. He answered, "Not tonight, Jean. But I'll get a cab for you."

An uncomfortable energy shifted between them as Jean muttered, "Never mind, David, don't bother. Good night." In an instant she disappeared from the club.

Mr. Belmont took Sarah's arm and they walked out onto the freshly dampened sidewalk. It had rained earlier, and the reflection of the street lamps and automobile headlights sparkled, mirror-like, on the black asphalt street. They laughed nervously, directionless and silent with anticipation. Her entire body felt like an electrical storm charged with spontaneous impulses, and as they stood in the wet, early morning shine, Mr. Belmont held Sarah in his arms and kissed her.

They took a cab to his apartment, and in the backseat she moved her body close to his. She watched the lamplight from the windows in the passing buildings, and wondered what worlds were opening up for other people, filled with the heat of new desire.

His apartment was dark. He turned on the jazz station, and while he poured himself a drink, asked if she wanted anything. The voice inside her head answered, "You, Mr. Belmont. I want you."

The music slipped through the room, and he held her close while they danced. She melted into his slow rhythm, and as one hand found the curve of her waist he brushed her hair away from her face with the other and brought her lips to his. Their kisses were long and deep. They sat on a large cushioned chair, and her eyes closed when his lips slid down her neck and his fingers unfastened the delicate pearl buttons on her dress.

He smelled like sweet powder. Her back arched as his arms wrapped around her, drawing her in, with no thought or reason in this entangled wilderness. They were caught in a web of seduction that tightened with every pull.

For so long she had wanted nothing more than this, but now that it was actually happening something was terribly wrong. Her body wasn't reacting. She pretended it was, and to force the numbness away she crushed herself against him. She started to breathe fast, as if there were no air in the room. Her chest tightened, and she moved to another couch.

"What is it, Sarah?" His voice was heavy.

"I can't, I just can't. I'm so sorry!" she gasped. He got up and came over to her, but she quickly slid to the other end.

Reaching for her, he said, "Look, I'm crazy about you."

She pulled away and stood up. "I can't." Her heart was pounding, and she felt sick to her stomach. She frantically looked for her coat and kept saying, "I'm sorry, really, I'm so sorry." When she rushed out she could hear the trail of his voice calling, "Sarah, what happened? Please, come back and talk to me!"

She got home and stood in front of her bathroom mirror feeling the loneliness that she so wanted to be saved from. She began to pace like the Siberian tiger in the Lincoln Park Zoo, and finally broke down in her closet, sobbing, clutching at her clothes. She picked up the telephone to call Karen but hung up after the first ring and packed two suitcases, got into her car and drove.

Later that afternoon she rented a studio apartment on the 10th floor of an old brown brick building on Lake Shore Drive. It was sparsely furnished, and the lake view was framed by three arched French doors that led to a small balcony. Sarah unpacked her belongings before pulling a chair onto the balcony to watch Lake Michigan swallow the evening sun.

The next morning she ate breakfast at a coffee shop around the corner. Sitting at the counter, she sensed something that she had never before experienced. From the very center of her fear came a feeling of power.

She spent the rest of the day shopping for odds and ends. She didn't want a television, but she did buy a CD player for her favorite music and her new Miles Davis disc. She took some time off from work, and for the next few days she kept a journal. Strangely enough, at night, she spoke out loud, imagining that Michael was listening to her, then, she'd curl her body around her pillow and cry herself to sleep.

On Tuesday morning, Sarah called Karen and an hour later they met in Lincoln Park. Dandelion fuzz drifted by as they walked through the damp, spring chill, but Sarah was too lost in her feelings to notice. She told Karen that she had come as close as she could have come to having an affair, but that her body wouldn't allow it as long as she was still committed to Michael. She knew it wasn't all his fault, but if Michael really wanted her, he was going to have to fight to keep her. She couldn't get past her own confusion, and when Karen put her arm around her on the gray park bench, Sarah broke down.

They held onto each other for a long time. Then Sarah faced Karen and said, "Michael's coming home tomorrow morning, and I want you to tell him everything that I just told you. I can't do it now and at this point I really don't want to know how he feels. I'm not ready to see him yet, and I don't want him to know where I live. Will you please do this for me, Karen?" Karen's hand tightened around Sarah's. "Of course, I will," she cried. "I'll do anything you want."

That night, lying in bed, Sarah knew that it wasn't really Mr. Belmont that she had wanted all this time. It was the feeling that she had inside her body when she thought of him, the freedom and excitement, the thrill of expectation and desire, but it wasn't him.

As the days passed, Sarah began to personalize her apartment. She even bought a sketchpad and started drawing. Sitting in front of the mirror, she drew her face carefully but her hand stopped at her eyes.

She moved in closer to find the secret behind them, and saw a darkness, an alienating darkness that Michael must have also seen.

Two weeks later she left word for Michael that she was ready to talk. Her Miles Davis tape was playing, and the room was filled with the delicate glow of sunset. The French doors were wide open, and a balmy breeze drifted through her apartment.

She smelled his cologne even before he knocked. Michael stood in front of the open door holding a bouquet of delicate, spring flowers. She could sense that he was scared to death of losing her and that the thought of her with another man was something that had never crossed his mind.

•   •   •

He stood on the platform in the spring rain in his three-piece suit holding his brown attaché case. His blond hair looked darker without the brightness and shine of the April sun. He waited for her every day, wondering what had happened that made Sarah vanish... like the passing trains at Belmont Station.

Sometimes in summer, I would ride the train all the way back home without transferring, just to pass through the different neighborhoods and look at the sun-dried clothes suspended from laundry lines that stretched across a maze of back porches. Black wrought iron fire escapes wrapped around red brick buildings, and table lamps or bare light bulbs spotted the passing windows at dusk. I'd watch families welcome the night sky on their front steps until it was time to tuck their children in and try to escape the stuffy humidity.

I wondered what it would be like to live in those neighborhoods where families spent time with each other, maybe out of necessity rather than want. Still, it was comforting to watch mothers sitting on stoops, wiping clean their children's sticky fingers or pushing the damp hair away from their faces. I saw love in their eyes as they stopped kids from fighting or bought them popsicles from the pushcart vendors in the dreamy afterglow of those summer evenings.

The light sprinkled under the downtown "el" tracks as if it were falling through lace curtains. Shadows streaked over unknowing faces that waited for buses or simply shuffled down the busy streets. Trees would umbrella over side streets as if they were protecting the kids riding bikes and gliding on roller skates. Muted colors of sunset cracked through clouds that looked like bunches of giant marbles, while the sun painted a cascade of orange, pink and yellow that echoed as far as the eye could see.

I'd watch newly married, romantic young couples walking arm in arm to the bus stops. Some would kiss their husbands goodbye as they boarded, then the look in their eyes would change and they'd walk back to their apartments, anxiously waiting for the day to pass so that they could be in the arms of their lovers again. It was different in my neighborhood, where I would hear husbands and wives arguing and yelling from various apartments in my building. What happened to those moments of wanting and waiting for deep kisses and falling into each other's arms?

SOMETHING IN COMMON

"I just don't want to live with you anymore, Eddie. You didn't do anything in particular, it's just over. What else can I say? I'm leaving you."

Standing in the middle of the living room of their small apartment, Ellen had the determined stance of a woman holding her ground, speaking with the confidence of someone much older than her 31 years. Her husband, Eddie, four years older, seemed childlike and insecure by comparison.

Eddie moaned, "I've noticed that you've been preoccupied and distant, but I had no idea it was this serious. What happened? I deserve to know! We gave seven years of our lives to each other. We were in love. I'm still in love with you, Ellen. Don't you still love me?"

Ellen had a blank expression on her face, but her deep, brown eyes showed her pain. Even after trying desperately to protect herself from her feelings, she still found him attractive. His sand-colored hair fell loosely onto his forehead, and from between the strands his smoky, gray eyes penetrated her and, if she allowed, could weaken her. Those eyes reminded her of the passion that had once simmered between them, but she knew those days were long gone, buried somewhere within her.

She took a deep breath before answering. "I'm sorry, Eddie, but I can't honestly say that I love you anymore. And, before your imagination runs wild, I'm not in love with anyone else either."

He stood motionless, confusion shadowing his angular face. "The thought of you being with someone else never even crossed my mind. Have you been seeing someone? All these years I've trusted you, and now I find out you've betrayed me?"

The veins on the side of his neck began to bulge. Ellen raised her voice, "I said that I am *not* seeing anyone, but I can guarantee you that I will be seeing someone, eventually." She resumed her natural tone, "But for now I just want to get to know myself. I don't expect you to understand, but you do deserve an explanation."

Eddie responded as if he hadn't heard a word. "So how long have you been seeing him?"

Ellen snapped, "This is one of my grievances. You don't listen! You never listen!" Her voice calmed. "But it isn't a grievance anymore because it's over." She walked to the hall closet to get a suitcase.

He interrupted her. "Uh, aren't you forgetting something?"

She stopped momentarily and eyed him suspiciously. "Is this a trick question?"

The color in his face changed and his agitation increased. "Our daughter? Have you even thought about Kristy while you've been sneaking around with your boyfriend? When did you plan on telling her that mommy and daddy went bye-bye?" His voice escalated. "Are you prepared to break her heart like you're breaking mine? No discussions, no trying to work out our problems. Just pack up your things and step over the broken pieces of your family on your way out!"

"It's so like you to play the victim," she blurted out. "This has absolutely nothing to do with Kristy. Where have you been, for Christ's sake? We haven't been a couple for a long time, and I've tried as much as I'm capable of trying. I'm not going to try to breathe life into something that I know is already dead, and I refuse to die with it!"

He sat on the pale green sofa with his shoulders hanging over his knees. His jeans were pressed but his T-shirt was wrinkled and wet from perspiration. The muscles in his arms were flexed with tension. Beaten down by this reality, his voice quivered. "You are so cruel. You talk as if you're the only one who's sacrificed for this relationship. I've sacrificed plenty, Ellen. If I had taken that other advertising job I would've had to travel one week out of every month and would've gotten home every night after Kristy had gone to bed. I didn't take it because I wanted to be with my family. I still do. Am I a bad provider? Am I not making enough money for you?" He punched the pillow on the couch and yelled, "Who's the guy you're seeing, damn it?"

"Oh, stop being so innocent." Her tone was laced with contempt. "I told you that we were in trouble a year ago, and don't blame it on our sex life. We both know we haven't had good sex in ages, but I still loved you. It wasn't the sex, or lack of. It was you. I can't live like this anymore, Eddie. I'm drying up. This is not the life I want, but that has nothing to do with Kristy. You've been an excellent father. You can see her anytime. I won't give you a problem with Kristy." Her voice softened, "Eddie, please, I don't know what pleasure you get from our being together. You must have felt the emptiness between us."

"Don't you dare tell me what I feel!" Eddie shouted, holding back his tears. "I have always felt love and devotion for you. How can you stop loving someone so fast? You're not telling me something, Ellen, I know it. You're dancing around the truth. I thought you were more of a person than this. Shame on you."

"Shame on me?" she cried. "Come on, Eddie, the only time I see you crack a smile is with Kristy. Other than that, you're always serious. If you haven't figured out how to have fun with me, then maybe it's time you figured it out with someone else."

Eddie straightened his body and pushed out his chest. He stood up and stretched his arms above his head. His hair fell over his eyes and the slightest hint of a smile curled the corners of his full lips. Indignantly, he replied, "I have had fun with someone else."

A puzzled expression crossed her face. "What are you saying?"

He stood his ground. "You call me serious, but there are plenty of people out there who are very attracted to me."

Ellen stood in the middle of the room, holding onto the empty suitcase until her voice cut through the silence. "You're lying. You're just saying that to hurt my feelings. You couldn't cheat on me."

She waited for a reaction, but none came. She walked to the window and stared down at the street. "When could you have possibly fit in an affair?" she asked. "You came home right after work, every night." When she swung her body around her dress flew up for an instant, exposing her thin, shapely legs. "Come on, Eddie, give me a little credit."

When he saw her legs a warm rush overcame him. Her petite figure could still excite him. The light in the room enhanced her delicate, porcelain skin, but there was fire burning in her dark eyes. "Who said it was an affair?" he said coolly, covering his desire for her.

"Why are you doing this? What's your point?" she asked.

He spoke as he sauntered around the room, "My point is honesty. If we're ending this, then it should end with the truth. Now I just told you I had fun with someone else. I said it. What have you said? Nothing. All you've said is that you're leaving me, but everything else is completely vague."

"What exactly do you mean by, 'fun with someone else?' Fun for you could be doing your taxes, for all I know. Did you have fun with your accountant? What kind of truth are you talking about, anyway?"

"I'll tell you if you tell me." He waited for an answer but no response came. "Are you even aware that this April we would have celebrated our seventh wedding anniversary, Ellen? We have a five-year-old child. We have a history between us. Laughter and tears. For better or for worse!"

"If you say sickness and health I'm going to throw up," she said sarcastically.

He moved closer to her. "I was going to say fighting and making up."

Ellen spoke calmly, "We're not going to make up, Eddie. I've made my decision. I want out. Whatever my reasons..."

"Well, what are they?" He pleaded. "That's all I'm asking! Come on, Ellen, tell me. Don't leave here like a stranger. You're my wife. Please, talk to me! I never abused or disrespected you. Why are you being so hurtful? I've always thought, at the very least, we were friends. Please, talk to me like I'm your friend."

Ellen turned away, her voice was low and distant. "You haven't been my friend for a long time, Eddie. I can hardly remember what it feels like to be close to you."

"Try, Ellen. Please try," he urged.

She sat on the windowsill, looking past the view, as if she were trying to remember a dream from long ago. "I know that I loved you terribly before we were married, and even after Kristy was born. Then, over a year ago, something changed. It wasn't a slow change either. It was like a shift, and suddenly things were different. Not bad. Not good. Just different. And they never snapped back. I waited, and then started getting used to the change. I noticed a distance, but so slight I didn't really know if it was you or me. You would say that it was PMS or being a mother or that I needed to work more. And I believed you, because I didn't want to believe that you weren't interested in me anymore. Or worse yet, that you weren't in love with me anymore."

"That's not true," Eddie interrupted. "I've always loved you. I still do."

The tone in her voice suddenly changed from concern to resignation. "I hear it, but I don't feel it. The man I love left me. I don't see any sense in having this conversation."

"No, please, please don't stop," he begged, "I want to hear what you have to say."

"Why, Eddie?" she asked. "What difference does it make? You're just going to deny it. Why should I set myself up? I already know what you're going to say."

"No, you don't. I can see your point of view." He was less defensive and more vulnerable as he spoke.

Ellen didn't notice the change and continued attacking. "Oh, really! All of a sudden you can see my point of view! What's different? Is it because you've admitted that you had fun with someone else?"

Eddie swallowed hard before he answered. "Maybe."

"Maybe! You mean you're serious?" she questioned. "You actually saw someone? Who? Do I know…?"

"It doesn't matter, Ellen, I just want to get to the truth. There's been so much denial and betrayal."

She looked confused. "Who's denying and betraying? What kind of words are these? Have you betrayed me, Eddie?"

Eddie looked down at the rug. He was pale and his forehead was moist. Ellen could hear the kitchen clock ticking from two rooms away as she waited for his answer. He finally responded. "Yes," he admitted. "Yes, Ellen, I've betrayed you."

Ellen sat down on the small ottoman in front of the coffee table where the family photos were placed. "When? When did you find the time? Who is she? Do I know her?" She shook her head in disbelief. "I can't believe this. How long has this been going on?"

Eddie spoke quietly, "For about a year and a half."

"You son of a bitch!" Ellen screamed. "You killed our marriage just for a thrill? What's the matter with you? Did I do something that--"

"It wasn't you, it was me," Eddie cried. "And it wasn't that often either. I want to be honest with you, Ellen. It happened at work. I felt so guilty about it. "

"Am I supposed to feel sorry for you for feeling guilty?" Ellen asked indignantly. "All this time I didn't trust my instincts. I was tormenting myself, blaming myself until I looked somewhere else for affection."

Silence filled the room.

Ellen dropped her head in her hands. The room was still. "I was never going to tell you this Eddie, never, but, I've been seeing someone for over a year."

He spoke as he stared at the photographs on the table. "Are you in love with him?"

"No. I'm not even sure if I like him," she chuckled. "Isn't that disgusting?"

"So you did betray me!" he snapped. "If I hadn't pushed you, you would have never told me." His voice cracked and he began to cry softly.

"God, what a mess," Ellen sighed. "Do I know her?" She asked.

"Yes."

"Would you please tell me who she is so that I don't invite her to lunch or something?"

Silence stood between them. "I don't think so."

"Come on, who is it, Eddie? Is it Kate?"

"No!" he cried. "I'm sorry, Ellen. I'm so sorry. I never wanted to hurt you."

"What's done is done. We're both in the wrong. Let's just lay all our cards on the table. No more secrets. We've come this far." Suddenly, Ellen jumped up. "I know! We'll both say the name of the person we've been sleeping with on the count of three. It'll be easier that way. Okay?"

"Oh, God. I don't think I can..." he muttered.

"Come on, Eddie," she urged. "It can't get any worse than it already is. We have nothing left to lose. Let's just do it. Air out our dirty laundry. Get it all out in the open so that we don't have to hold on to anything anymore. No more lies, no more secrets. No more guilt. We'll both start fresh. Okay? Okay, Eddie?"

Eddie looked troubled, but Ellen was fueled by the excitement of confessing their sins and being free of the guilt. She was talking fast. "Alright. Here we go. On the count of three, Eddie, we'll both say the names of our lovers out loud, and that will be it. On the count of three. Okay? One," Eddie began to fidget.

"Two," their eyes locked.

"Three! Say it!" she screamed.

Simultaneously, they said, "STUART!"

Disbelief covered their faces as they looked at each other from opposite ends of the room. Eddie clutched his hands to his stomach and began to laugh. Ellen dropped the suitcase and crossed the room to sit on the sofa. Roars of Eddie's laughter bellowed throughout their apartment as he fell back on the couch.

Ellen was searching her mind. She was lost in memory. "How could this be? Do you hate me that much or... or... are you gay?"

Eddie's laughter ended. He answered without looking at her. "Yes."

"Yes, you're gay, or yes, you hate me?"

"Yes, I'm gay," he said softly.

Things looked the same. The sun still lit the spring sky. The room they were in was exactly as it had always been, but now everything was different. Ellen's mind raced through the years they had spent together. She felt humiliated and numb.

Her teeth crushed together and she closed her eyes before asking, "Are you HIV-positive? Do you have AIDS?"

"No," he answered quickly.

She muttered under her breath, "Do I have...?" Then she turned to Eddie and asked, "Is Stuart HIV-positive?"

Eddie answered firmly, "No. He's been tested, and we always practiced safe sex. Didn't you?"

"Do you really think I'm going to tell you about my sexual habits with *your* lover?" she gasped. "God, I can't fathom this. Did you know that Stuart was bisexual, 'cause I certainly didn't! Is he your first? Why did you marry me, Eddie? Our marriage has been falling apart, and in one afternoon I'm leaving, you're gay and we're both fucking the same guy! Where's the punch line? Are we on 'Candid Camera' or something, because this certainly feels like a big joke! I can't believe you lied to me all this time!"

"I lied to myself, Ellen," Eddie cried. "I've always felt the attraction but never acted on it. If Stuart hadn't pushed me so hard I might have never acted on it, although it still would have been there, inside me. I loved you then, and I love you now. I always will. I don't want you to leave, but if you have to I want to free you from blaming yourself. You were right. When I started with Stuart I did move away from you emotionally and physically, but it had nothing to do with you. It was me. It was all me. God, I've ruined everything."

Eddie began to sob. He tried to talk, but his words were unintelligible. Ellen moved closer to him. "I can't understand what you're saying, Eddie." She put her hand on his shoulder and waited for him to calm down. "The thing that's really strange is that Stuart knew all along, and we didn't. I'm so embarrassed. He must have known we'd find out some day."

Eddie settled down before answering. "Stuart promised that he'd never tell anyone about us, and he knew that I'd never tell you. I told him that I loved you and never wanted you to know."

Ellen kept her hand on Eddie's shoulder. She wanted answers to the questions that were shooting through her mind. "How long could you have gone on like this? Why on earth did you want to marry me?"

Eddie put his hand on Ellen's lap as he spoke. "I love you, Ellen. I want to spend the rest of my life with you and Kristy. I find you completely desirable, but I'm attracted to men in a different way. It doesn't mean that I'm not attracted to you. You're my best friend in the world. I've always told you everything, except for this one thing. It's the only secret I've ever kept from you. I hope to God you believe that."

Ellen brushed the hair from his forehead. "This isn't a secret, Eddie. This is who you are. I didn't marry you for friendship."

Taking her hand, he said, "For better or worse."

She dropped his hand and turned away. "This is beyond worse. I have no chance here. If I had known this from the start, I would have never given my heart to you. I made a lifetime commitment based on a lie. What a shame this is."

Ellen stood up and began to walk across the room. Eddie grabbed the hem of her dress to stop her. "You're right about everything," he said. "I wish I could change it, but I can't. I'm afraid, Ellen. It was easier to hide. You and Kristy are the best things in my life, and I'm losing both of you. Oh, please forgive me. Please forgive me for hurting you."

He let go, and she sat near him. "You know, it's strange," she said. "I have a crystal clear point of view at this moment. Maybe this is the eye of the storm. It's like this is not happening to me, and I genuinely feel sorry for you, Eddie. I actually want to help you. It's funny."

"If you really want to help me, Ellen, then say you forgive me."

Ellen embraced Eddie, and he began to sob again. Her eyes saddened and she also began to cry.

"I forgive you, Eddie," she whispered.

They held onto each other until Eddie stopped crying. He looked into her eyes and took her face in his hands and gently kissed her. "Thank you," he said.

He kissed her again with passion, and when they released Ellen kept her eyes closed as she stood up. Then, she looked at him one last time and simply turned and walked out the front door, never looking back, as Eddie sat on the end of the couch, staring at her empty suitcase.

As a young girl, when I would come home, I'd close the door to my room and sing. I'd sing with Anita O'Day, June Christy, and Ruth Olay. Love songs, sad songs. Nina Simone, Carmen McRae, *Judy Garland at Carnegie Hall*. Frank Sinatra. *Each place I go, only the lonely go.* I would play that album all night long. I'd listen to Sid McCoy on WCFL, the midnight jazz station. *"Hey, hey old bean, and you too, baby. It's the Real McCoy."*

Music was my friend. It was the ear that listened to me. It embraced and comforted me. I was in love with music. It charged me up or made me weep. I could always count on it to bring out my truest feelings.

When I heard Barbra Streisand's first album, it was life-changing for me. The material, the amazing arrangements and orchestrations, the lyrics, her unique interpretations and that powerful, emotional, dramatic voice. Those songs crawled inside me. I sang with her day and night. She was singing what I was feeling, and I was feeling so much. I was home.

I understood myself when I sang. I belonged in the middle of those chord changes. I was alive. My life needed a soundtrack, and it was in my young, romantic head following me wherever I'd go.

Other than my neighbor Jackie, no one knew that I sang except for my parents, and they only knew because I lived with them. I'd look outside my bedroom window at the telephone wires and backyards that lined the alley and sing to the changing seasons. *"Autumn, it feels like autumn."* How I loved to sing. *"Love me, love me, say you do."* I wasn't alone anymore.

I sang with Nancy Wilson and Cannonball Adderley. I loved Gil Evans arrangements because of the strangeness that strangled the horn section. I sang along with instrumental solos by Miles Davis, Bill Evans, Lee Morgan, Horace Silver and Stan Getz, and at breakneck speed with Lambert, Hendricks and Ross. *"I sat, one night, right in the middle of a glass of Coca-Cola."*

I loved cool jazz, but when folk rock came, it added a new dimension. Bob Dylan and Joan Baez. Buffy Sainte-Marie and Ronnie Gilbert. Protest songs and real poetic anger. I bought a steel-stringed guitar for $5 and a friend of mine taught me some chords and strums, and I wrote a bunch of songs with only three or four of the same chords. Now the words were mine. I didn't need albums to sing with anymore, I could accompany myself. I sat on my bed for hours making up words and melodies with the same chord changes. Holding the guitar so close to my body helped to comfort me.

I'd ride the "el" to Rush Street or Old Town just to be close to creative energy. Maybe I wasn't really a part of it yet, but at least I was in the neighborhood. Only a few of my friends would come with me, but they usually felt out of place there. I was totally comfortable. It was the only place I wanted to be. I never told anyone that I sang. I would have been too embarrassed to sing in front of people or to put someone in the uncomfortable position of feeling obligated to respond. Singing was a sacred space. It was holy to me.

THE PROFESSOR

"It doesn't flow," she said. You know what I mean?"

The Professor listened. He was used to these abstract explanations. For over a year she had been forcing out a shallow, uncontrollable sound that took all the joy out of singing. She had been a professional recording and performing artist for more than 15 years, but now the sound was no longer coming from her heart. It was coming from her throat.

"Just tell me what I'm doing wrong!" the woman pleaded. "Is it my breathing? Are the years that I smoked catching up with me? My throat doctor said I don't have nodes, so what do you think it could be?"

She was asking the Professor because his reputation as a vocal coach was flawless and she wanted to believe that he could help her.

"Even if I told you," he replied, "you couldn't do anything about it."

Silence filled his office. "You mean you know what I'm doing wrong, and you're not going to tell me?" Her mind was moving fast, trying to figure out how to manipulate the answer from him.

Sensing her desperation, he calmly said, "You're tensing up your throat when you sing."

"Yeah?"

"Yeah."

"So?"

"So, that's it."

"That's it? I'm tensing up! No kidding!"

"I told you that you wouldn't be able to do anything about it," he said. "First, you have to do my exercises, and everything else will follow. You must remember that your entire body is the instrument."

She eyed him intently. "How long will it take?"

"I don't know. It's different for each person."

"*About* how long?"

He met her gaze. "Believe me, I understand how important this is to you, but you have years of bad habits to unlearn. It's not going to happen overnight."

Even though he appeared to be about 75, his energy was that of a younger man, and there was a fixed kindness in his eyes. She had a feeling that he could help her if she were patient. Patience wasn't one of her virtues, but one thing was certain. She was willing to do anything to sing again.

"Now what?" she asked.

"Now we'll start," he said firmly. The Professor gave her some vocal exercises that made her sound awful. "This isn't music," he stressed. "These are simply to help balance the muscles. Think of them only in that way. If you get a sound, fine. If you don't, fine. Just do them once a day, and I'll see you next week if you want."

"But I thought I would see you everyday!" she blurted out.

"Do the exercises for a week, then come back, and we'll have something to talk about."

There was an ease about him, and she sensed that he let life take him where it was going, unlike the constant willful storms that stirred inside her. She didn't want to wait a whole week to see him again, but reluctantly agreed.

She was startled awake from a nightmare, and the images were still vivid. She was in her dressing room getting ready to do a concert when there was a knock at the door. A voice called, "Five minutes, please." She rushed to finish her makeup but it wouldn't stick to her skin. Hearing the restless audience, she ran on stage before anyone announced her. The musicians began to play the opening number and at that very moment she forgot all the words.

The band kept playing, and when she finally remembered the lyrics she opened her mouth, but not a single sound came out. She had no voice. The concert hall lights dimmed and she moved closer to the edge of the stage to see the audience, only to discover the hall was empty. She turned to the band, and they were all gone. Suddenly, everything was dripping wet. It was raining inside the auditorium. She was afraid of being electrocuted because she was standing in puddles of water while holding the live microphone. That's when she woke up.

She was 36 years old and knew that she would be crushed if she couldn't sing anymore. After splashing water on her face she saw that her eyes showed the loneliness and terror she so desperately wanted to wash away.

In her den she looked at the Professor's exercises on the music stand. For the past week she had been doing them religiously, pushing out screechy little noises that made her sound like a train making an emergency stop. At times they were so piercing that she would actually hold her fingers in her ears while doing them. The Professor had told her to practice only once a day, but, thinking she'd speed up the process, she was up to three times a day. Her manager was pressing for a European tour, but she wanted to hold off until spring, hoping that by then she'd be ready.

She spent the morning cleaning her apartment until it was time for her lesson. She walked briskly to the Professor's office and, once there, took the elevator to the fourth floor and stood in the outer hall waiting for the singing lesson that was in progress to end. Since the exercises made everyone sound so awful, it was almost impossible to know which of the Professor's students were professionals. The door opened, and a depressed-looking student came out and smiled weakly at her.

The Professor greeted her and asked if she'd been practicing.

"Of course." she answered, as she passed him to enter his office. "I practice three times a day."

He frowned. "But I told you to do the exercises only once a day."

She nodded, saying, "Yes, but if I do them more often I'll build up my stamina and break through faster."

"That's not how it works. Aren't you hoarse?" he asked.

She looked surprised, "Yes I am, as a matter of fact, but I thought I was just catching a cold."

His rhythm was steady as he spoke. "You aren't catching a cold. You're trying too hard." Nothing about him was punishing, and even though his voice was slow and sympathetic, she needed him to understand that she didn't have time to go slowly. She was in a hurry to sing.

After her lesson, the Professor put on his overcoat and wrapped his wool scarf around his neck. When he reached for his Russian hat, she asked where he was going.

"I'm going to have lunch at a Chinese restaurant near here," he replied.

"Are you meeting someone?" she asked.

He seemed to sense her loneliness. "No," he said. "Would you like to join me? It's not fancy or anything. It's just a place that I like."

She had always been impressionable, and she hoped that the more time she spent with him the more he would rub off on her. She grabbed her coat and they headed out together.

His feet flopped on the pavement and he tipped slightly forward when he walked, as if an invisible string were pulling him to his destination. His demeanor was warm, yet laced with distance, but she was confident the distance would disappear the more they got to know each other.

People sitting at the bar greeted the Professor as they entered the dark restaurant. They sat in a booth in the back, and he ordered a scotch and soda. She was suddenly struck with the strangest sensation. Her entire body felt as if it were tingling on the inside. She was simultaneously hot and cold and was acutely aware of her racing heart. A wave of nausea came over her, and for a moment, she thought she was going to throw up.

Unaware of what she was feeling, the Professor lightly touched her hand. "So tell me about yourself," he said. The heat from his hand surged through her. When she looked into his eyes she couldn't hold back her tears. It took some time before she settled down. Finally, her body relaxed and her eyes opened as if she were awakening from a strange dream. The entire time the Professor held onto her hand, never saying a word. "What's happening?" she asked.

"I don't know. Why are you so sad?"

With her face streaked with tears, she said, "I'm not sad."

His free hand extended his handkerchief. "Usually when people cry they're sad about something, but maybe you cry for different reasons. The ice cubes in your water have melted. Would you like another?"

Feeling stunned, she looked down at the puddle around her glass. The Professor was watching her.

"I'm so sorry!" she gushed. "This has never happened to me. I don't even know why I started crying! I hope I didn't embarrass you."

He squeezed her hand, and again she felt the warmth flow through her. "They weren't my tears," he said. "They were yours. I'm fine." That's what she envied about him. He wasn't the victim of his surroundings or circumstances. He was whole within himself. In touch with what was and what wasn't his.

She had always thought of herself as a leader, but now she was feeling like a woman who needed to be led. She was lost, and felt helpless and filled with the terror of never being able to sing again. For her, singing was much more than just making music. If she couldn't sing, it would be an amputation of what connected her to life. It wasn't desire. It was necessity.

A few weeks later, while doing the Professor's exercises, she became distracted by a flowerpot that looked as if it were about to blow off her windowsill. She reached for it while continuing the exercise and she hit a high note so easily that it startled her. It simply flowed out. Effortlessly. She immediately called the Professor. She told him that she hadn't been thinking or even trying for that matter. He said, "Remember the feeling." That's all he said.

She continued her studies, hanging on to his every word. He was her guide for now. She had bonded with him and her studies became her sole pursuit. She was getting results, creating a new routine and breaking old, bad habits. It was working.

One evening she went for a walk and found herself wandering a few blocks from the Chinese restaurant where she had gone with the Professor. It began to rain, and she decided to stop in for a drink. Before entering, she glanced in the window. She stood outside, motionless.

The Professor was sitting at the bar with a young woman who appeared to be in her 20s. The woman's arms were wrapped around the Professor's neck, while his hand rested seductively just below her waist. Occasionally they would kiss in a short burst of passion and then release in a rush of laughter. She was surprised to see him in this manner, but what confused her most was a feeling of overwhelming jealousy.

She walked back to her apartment in the rain and collapsed in a deep sleep on her living room couch. The next morning she woke up in soggy clothes with a sore throat and a deep chest cough. It was so unlike her to risk getting sick. Singers are notoriously paranoid about illness, but this morning she didn't even think about her throat. She was preoccupied with thoughts of the Professor and the woman in the restaurant. She had a singing lesson later that afternoon, and because she didn't feel well she would normally cancel, but there was no way she was going to break today's appointment.

They couldn't do anything since her vocal chords were sore. "I thought we could work around it," she said.

"Work around what?" the Professor asked. She had such intensity in her eyes that he walked over to her and asked if anything was wrong. She threw herself at him, burying her face in his chest and clinging tightly to him. He stood still with his arms hanging loosely at his side. A moment later she let go.

"I went for a walk last night and passed the Chinese restaurant where we had lunch. I saw you with a woman. Is she your girlfriend?"

"Yes," he answered.

She pushed some papers off a wooden chair and sat down. He sat beside her and quietly said, "I'm not sure I know what's going on."

She was bewildered too, sitting motionless, staring at her shoes. The Professor moved closer. She didn't say a word. She felt totally exposed, as though her skin had been meticulously peeled from her body, but oddly enough her throat felt better.

Finally she spoke. "I don't know what's wrong with me lately. I've been so sensitive and emotional, and this may sound strange, but I feel somehow abandoned."

"You're right," he said. "You have been abandoned."

Turning to him, her eyes welled up with tears, " By who?" she questioned.

"By your voice," he answered. "And now that you don't have it, you feel lost."

She covered her face with her hands. "Everything was fine until this thing started with my voice," she cried. "Maybe I should just stop singing altogether."

The Professor's face changed, and it was as if the room had darkened. He became very serious. This was a side of him that she hadn't seen before. "Listen to me. I've worked with the creative spirit all my life," he said. "Your voice is trying to tell you something. If you don't face this now, I'm not sure you'll have another chance."

His tone frightened her. "Another chance at what?" she questioned.

His eyes were fixed on her. "At life." He put on his winter coat and walked out of the office. She grabbed her coat and raced after him. While they waited for the elevator, he adjusted his scarf and hat. She stood behind him and without looking at her, he said, "Let's go for a drink."

They took the same back booth in the Chinese restaurant. It was easier for her to talk facing him, instead of being distracted by the rows of bottles and customers at the bar.

"When did you start to sing?" he asked.

"Before I could talk," she said. "I was around two years old, and I would sing with all the radio commercials. My mom got a big kick out of it. Then I discovered old Judy Garland records and I sang with her all the time."

He asked if she was in talent shows at school. She shook her head. "Oh, no. No one knew that I could sing except my parents. I never told anyone."

The Professor looked surprised. "Then how did you become a professional singer?"

She looked down at her drink and moved her finger in the water droplets on the table, tracing patterns as she spoke. "A friend of mine who worked as a waitress at a nightclub came over one day and caught me singing in my room. She couldn't believe I had never told her that I could sing. She brought me to the nightclub on a Monday night when anyone could perform on stage. She kept putting these sweet creamy drinks in front of me. I must have had about four of them before she introduced me to a guy who she said was going to play guitar that night. She said he wanted me to teach him the chords to a song I knew. I was too drunk to realize what was actually happening."

The Professor watched and listened. A slight smile covered his face as she continued. "It was after midnight when I heard my name echoing through the club. My friend gently pushed me toward the stage, and the guitar player was sitting there. I was so confused, but the next thing I knew I was standing in the middle of the stage singing the song I had just taught him to play."

Her eyes were closed and it was as if she were watching her memories fleeting by on a secret screen in her mind. "When I left the stage, a club owner from down the street came up to me and asked if I would like to sing at his place for $30 a night for the next two weekends. I couldn't believe someone would actually pay me to sing. Then another man approached me and said he wanted to manage me, but by that time my head was spinning. I worked for the two weekends and was held over for two more. On the last night, I was discovered by an agent who offered me a record deal, and my career took off. That was 15 years ago."

"So you're a natural talent. You didn't study formally and never auditioned for anyone."

"Yes." she said. "That's true."

"Then trust your talent. It's trying to teach you something now. Don't fight it. Embrace it. Follow it."

She looked at him with wide eyes. "But where will it lead me?"

"Wherever you're supposed to go," he answered.

Over the next few weeks she thought about what the Professor had said. It rang true for her. "Stop thinking so much," he'd say. "Art is intuitive. Thinking will block it. Get out of the way and just let it happen."

That was true. Singing and music had always been about feeling. Not to say that she didn't analyze and work on trying new approaches, but in order to satisfy herself, and interpret the lyric, she had to be free enough to feel the music.

A story would appear in her mind as if she were watching a film, where she was both the main character and the storyteller. That's why working on arrangements was so important to her. They were the emotional soundtrack to the story. If the arrangement didn't express how she saw the song, then it didn't work. The words and the music had to become one, then the lyric would always direct the mood.

But now she couldn't express the lyric because her voice wasn't free and was holding her back. She couldn't feel the music anymore because all of her attention was on her voice. It was as if she were walking barefoot on a beach covered with sharp rocks.

The Professor reeled her back to the lyric. He got her to stop thinking about the rocks, and breathe in the salt air. "Breathe. Breathe and relax," he'd say. And he would squeeze his eyes shut for an instant and smile. "Don't think. That's your biggest problem," he said over and over again. Her attention was on her brain, not on her heart.

But there were some familiar spurts of that warm, suspended rush that would come from her heart and move through her body that had nothing whatsoever to do with her brain. It would happen spontaneously, and she noticed it more and more with every lesson. When setbacks occurred, she would wonder if she would ever again be able to feel the surge of creativity that used to come so naturally.

She walked into her apartment and immediately saw the red light blinking on her answering machine. The recorded voice was frantic. "It's Joey. Oh God, I hope you're in town! My singer was in a minor car accident, and it's too late to cancel this gig, and you know all the material. If you have any feeling for me at all, you'll meet me at Mother Blues in Old Town at 8:45. Please, please, don't let me down!"

Beads of perspiration dotted her forehead. She looked at the time. It was almost 7:00 p.m. Her first instinct was to call and say she couldn't do it. She thought, "Oh no, not now! Not when I'm having all this trouble!" She put her hands over her ears to block the argument screaming inside her. Then she dressed and caught a cab to Old Town.

When Joey saw her, all the anxiety drained from his face. She peeked at the audience from the side of the stage. Every seat was taken. She kept telling herself to feel the music. Then, the announcer introduced the group, and when the crowd heard that she was the guest vocalist they went wild. She stepped onstage, and the intro to the opening song vamped on until Joey nodded for her to start.

At that very moment she felt a cold chill shoot through her, and her eyes flooded with panic. She had forgotten the words. She was sure that everyone could hear her heart pounding over the sound system. Then

Joey shouted her name, and she closed her eyes, stopped thinking, and sang.

Notes flew out of her. She was lost in the music. In every song. She was home again. The crowd was on their feet. After the show, people poured backstage. Some told her that no one else could have touched them so deeply. The band took her out to celebrate until early morning light cracked the evening sky. Still wide awake, she was desperate to talk to the Professor.

She climbed the stairs to his apartment, apologizing all the way up for bothering him so early on a Saturday morning. He stood in his doorway in his robe and slippers. "It's okay," he said. "What happened?"

He stood with his arms wrapped around his body, laughing as she spoke, when suddenly, the breeze blew open the door to his apartment. The young woman she'd seen him with at the Chinese restaurant was standing inside. She was wearing a white flannel nightgown, and the bright light behind her backlit the silhouette of her shapely body. She had thick red hair, and was prettier than she had looked in the restaurant. She smiled warmly, urging them to come in, out of the cold. Then she excused herself and left them alone.

In the kitchen of his small apartment, the Professor asked her to go on with her story. She continued excitedly, and when she finished, she looked into his eyes.

He smiled and said, "Remember the feeling."

When she got home, she fell into a deep sleep, and when she awoke she called her manager to book the European tour.

During the next 10 years she sang all over the world. She kept in touch with the Professor, calling him from different countries and sometimes wouldn't even mention singing. She'd just want to hear his voice. He was always warm and patient with her. They both knew that now she was connected to the music that played from inside of her.

It was while she was on tour in Japan, as the cherry blossoms opened their delicate pink petals, that she received a telegram that the Professor had died. She cancelled the tour and took the first flight home.

It was a perfect spring day. There were more than 200 people, from all over the world, at the funeral. Throughout the ceremony everyone reminisced about how important the Professor had been to them and how much they loved him. It was clear that it was going take a long time to adjust to life without him. After the ceremony, they all decided to meet at the Chinese restaurant to continue to comfort each other.

She sat in her car until everyone had gone and then walked back to his gravesite. Little yellow dandelions spotted the vibrant green grass. She stood motionless, longing to find a way to say goodbye. She sensed the grace around her. Then she stopped to listen to the voice inside her heart. It simply said, "Remember the feeling."

It was a normal Saturday afternoon with thick Chicago humidity hanging in the hot summer air. My older brother, Richard, was coming to pick me up at 9:30 a.m. in front of the Drake Hotel to visit our Uncle Eddie, my father's brother, who was ailing with a heart condition. I had flown in from L.A. just to visit him, and was worried that this might be the last time I would see my favorite uncle.

I was early and had time to buy a flower arrangement at the hotel florist. I asked the salesperson to remove all the carnations from the setting because their scent reminded me of death and funerals. He replaced them with purple orchids and white calla lilies. It took a little longer than I had planned and I was late to meet my brother, but he was cheerful as usual, happy to be with me.

We laughed and talked our way to the West Side and found a parking spot right in front of Uncle Eddie's apartment building. Eddie was sick. Congestive heart failure, emphysema, rheumatoid arthritis. He couldn't walk anymore. I remembered him as a giant of a man who looked more like my father than my father.

He was sitting in a big chair by the window of his small apartment. The afternoon light changed often, and I could see the leaves on top of the big shady maple tree outside dancing in the summer breeze. Rain was forecast, and the room felt as if it were slowly revolving from the shifting light and shadows. Eddie was happy to see us. His eyes twinkled as he told stories packed with memories and lost relatives and about my father and him as children. We connected, and that's all I could have asked for.

Three hours later, as my brother and I walked to the car, I asked if he knew where our father's father was buried. He knew the cemetery and somehow remembered that the grave was by a big catalpa tree. The Russian Orthodox cemetery had beautiful rolling lawns with huge trees shading graves that were well over a hundred years old. Entire families were buried beside each other, with empty plots waiting nearby to welcome the next relative. Crosses of all sizes outlined the horizon. Some graves had small buildings on top of them, others had flat tombstones on the ground, but all were well kept and sunlight sprinkled everywhere.

At the main office we learned our grandfather's grave was in the middle of the cemetery. My brother was right about the catalpa tree. His tombstone was flat on the grass, and his oval photograph was embedded in the stone. No relatives were around him. He was surrounded by green, damp grass.

All my life my father told me violent stories about his father. But now, as I stood over my grandfather's grave, I forgave him for mistreating my father as a child. Suddenly, I felt sorry that my father missed having the father he wanted. And here I was, speaking to my dead grandfather, a stranger, praying for his soul. I kissed my fingers and placed them on his oval picture before leaving.

"Now where do you want to go?" my brother asked.

"I want to go and see mom's parents. Do you know where they're buried?" I wondered aloud.

My maternal grandparents were buried in one of the oldest, and smallest, Jewish Orthodox cemeteries in the city, which had merged with 200 other cemeteries. The main office said that they were in a remote section. Their particular plot was six graves wide and two lots deep. Very old. Very narrow. There was no entrance, just an old gate locked with a rusty chain.

As we walked from the car, a truck with three workers was pulling out of a side entrance that we decided to enter. My eyes followed, suspiciously, to see if the truck would turn onto the thoroughfare. It occurred to me that this was a prime situation for foul play. We were two unprotected people walking into an isolated and desolate area, and if someone had bad intentions, we were the perfect victims. The thought of my brother and I being murdered and quickly buried crossed my mind. We were already in a cemetery. No one would think twice about seeing someone dig a fresh grave, and no one on earth would have ever found us because no one on earth knew where we were. We would have been lost forever, covered by the same soil as our ancestors. The truck disappeared down the highway. This is the imagination I inherited.

THE RINGING BELLS

In the middle of a heated argument with her husband, Eve suddenly stopped and walked out. She simply got into her car and drove north up Pacific Coast Highway until she noticed that her gas gauge was almost on empty. The highway was also empty. Only an occasional delivery truck roared by. She filled her tank and drove on until the sun woke the morning sky.

Toward late morning she started getting drowsy and stopped at a roadside inn. She wasn't very hungry, opting for a piece of cherry pie and a cup of tea before renting a room with an ocean view. The room was stark with no air conditioning, but a ceiling fan kept the summer air moving. Eve opened the window, but there was no breeze coming off the ocean.

"The ozone layer," she mumbled to herself. "It's screwing up the climate." There was a time when she could always count on an ocean breeze. The fresh, cool wind would stimulate her and, somehow, make her feel healthier. Now, brown smog hung over the water like a dirty gauze curtain, and the foam in the surf bubbled like detergent. She closed the faded green drapes and placed her dress on an old bureau before dropping onto the bed. The mattress had no box spring to cushion her body, but she was sleeping before she even noticed that there were no pillows on the bed.

Her dreams were, more or less, the same as they had been for the last year or so. She was used to the frightening images that haunted her sleep and the restless anxiety that caused her to wake up every 30 to 40 minutes. She didn't want to understand the symbols. All she knew was that she had no peace. It wasn't clear to her if the knocking was part of her nightmare or if it were real, but whatever the realm, it awakened her. No peace.

"Who is it?" Eve whispered.

"Maid service, Miss."

Eve angrily replied, "Go away!"

"There was no sign on your doorknob ma'am. Sorry."

There was no sign on the doorknob because there was no sign in the room to hang on the doorknob, but, by now, Eve was on her back with her eyes wide open wondering how long she'd slept. She pulled the drapes open just in time to see the Pacific Ocean swallow the sun.

The bathroom's fluorescent light made a buzzing sound that annoyed her so much that she turned it off and took a shower in the dark. She put on the same clothing, and with her hair still wet, checked out of the Inn without looking back. Yet she knew she would never forget the brief time she had spent there.

"I'd like to report a missing person," Brian said. "My wife's been gone since late last night... I have to wait 24 hours to file a report? Don't you think I'd know if my wife was missing or not?" He paused. "Well then, it's lucky I have an ocean view. I'll call you when I see her body floating by."

He slammed down the phone so hard it made his ears ring. If he hadn't stopped smoking four years earlier he would have lit one up right now, breathing in deeply, and letting the smoke linger a while in his lungs before releasing it back into the stale air of the room.

He couldn't stop thinking about Eve. He had noticed that she'd been overwhelmed lately and couldn't handle too much. He hadn't taken it very seriously, and thought it was some female thing. But now he felt he should have been more interested. Not that he wasn't sensitive to her. He most definitely was, but not all the time. He would occasionally flirt with other women at parties, but that's as far as it went. He was willingly faithful, and loved his wife.

But lately the temptation grew stronger because sex was almost a dead issue between them. They were an affectionate and romantic couple, but she would freeze up when he made more aggressive advances. They had openly discussed it, and she had been genuinely confused by her own reaction. She had talked about it with her gynecologist, thinking that she might be going through an early menopause, even though she was only in her mid-30s. A series of tests showed slight indications, but nothing significant. Brian knew that it wasn't the sex. He could live without sex. But he could never consider living without Eve.

She drove north all day, stopping just once for a quick sandwich at a truck stop diner. It was as if she had stepped back in time, sitting at the counter with the jukebox playing a country song by Conway Twitty. As a young girl she used to like Conway Twitty. Country music wasn't that popular when she was growing up in Chicago, and now Conway Twitty was singing in this roadside dive, and she was sad that he had died and would never sing again.

"Hey baby, can I buy you another cup of something? Where you headed?" She turned to the guy hanging over her right shoulder. He had bad breath and his eyes were bloodshot from either drinking too much or not getting enough sleep, and she had no intention of knowing which it was.

"Which question do you want me to answer first?" she said, while leaving a tip on the counter.

"Any one you feel like, honey," he said, moving in closer.

She stood and faced him. "The first answer is no, and the second is, none of your fucking business." Then she smiled and said, "Have a nice day."

Eve slammed the car door harder than she wanted to. The force hurt her arm, but that wasn't all that was hurting. Her unhappiness made her ache all over. When she stopped earlier for gasoline, she went to the restroom and started crying, and she knew her heart had a lot more crying to do.

She was sad. Sad at the way the world was turning out. Sad for endangered species. Sad for the homeless, and sad that she was so sad. She knew it wasn't anyone's fault that she couldn't find happiness, it just wasn't there. She'd looked to Brian for comfort and support, but he hadn't filled her need, and she felt so guilty putting him through her mood swings. She'd often wondered how long he would hang in with her. She sleepwalked through days, sometimes weeks. She couldn't connect. Everything overwhelmed her. Life confused her.

Night was falling. She had driven out of California, and was passing surrounding forests seeing fleeting glimpses of wildlife in the dimming light. Suddenly, her car headlights flashed on a large deer, with great pointed antlers. It reared back, and she momentarily lost control of the car and swerved off the road.

As she gathered herself from this near accident, a young woman, who appeared to come out of nowhere, ran up to her window. The suddenness of the woman's appearance made Eve jump up and hit her head on the roof of the car. Eve opened the door for some fresh air, breathing deeply. There wasn't a sound.

The woman's voice broke through the silence. "Are you okay? I have a first aid kit in my backpack. It's not a big deal, a bandage, an aspirin, stuff like that, but it's better than nothing. My name is Angie."

Eve looked up and smiled. "Thanks, but I think I'm fine. I just hit my head. I was more startled than anything. Although I may need that aspirin. I'm Eve."

"Well, Eve, it looks like we're all alone out here," Angie said. "I was just hitching further up north. I don't know how far you're going, but if you'd like some company, I could sure use the ride."

This is the kind of situation that Eve would never go for. Hitchhikers were a definite "no" on her safety scale. Even if she saw a little kid or an old lady thumbing a ride, it was absolutely out of the question. She didn't trust anyone she didn't know. It was a given.

"Sure. Hop in," she said. Eve leaned over to unlock the passenger side. There was something about this young woman's presence that made Eve feel safe.

"Say Eve, if you need to rest, I'd be glad to drive for a while," Angie offered. "I'm used to driving on winding roads in forest country. How about it?"

Eve responded by crawling into the back seat. "Sure, I could use a break," she said. There it was again. Eve would have never dreamt of letting anyone touch her car, let alone drive it, but at this moment she was relieved to not have the responsibility of driving. She felt cared for. Enough so that she fell asleep moments after Angie pulled away.

Angie was small, but her clothes were enormous. A large, rust-colored flannel shirt hung almost to her knees, which were covered by baggy brown sweats. Her beat-up hiking boots looked as though they weighed more than she did, and she tossed her old backpack on the floor.

When Eve opened her eyes, all that she could see out the window were trees lit by the full moon above. She looked at Angie and saw a very pretty young woman who appeared to be in her early 20s, with a small nose and skin that was luminous, flush with a pale pink glow. Her large, curious brown eyes scanned the highway, and the corners of her mouth pulled up, ever so slightly, adding a friendly warmth to her face. Her hands steadily held the steering wheel, and her fingernails had dirt under them as if she had been digging in the ground.

Her golden hair was shoulder length, curled at the ends and pulled off of each side of her face by two pointy barrettes. Some of the curls were in little ringlets that bounced as they went over the bumps in the road, and with each bump Eve heard a gentle ringing sound that came from Angie's silver bracelet. There were two tiny bells attached to it, and the sound was like a baby's toy, soft and delicate. Angie knew that Eve was awake but didn't talk until Eve broke the silence.

"Does the ringing from your bracelet ever bother you, Angie?" Eve asked.

"No. Never. It reminds me that angels are always near," she answered.

Eve smiled to herself at such a sweet image.

"How long was I out for?" Eve asked.

"I wasn't timing it, but I'd guess around 45 minutes or so. Where are you coming from, Eve?" Angie's voice was calm and friendly. Eve liked its sound.

"L.A."

"I don't like L.A. Too populated for me."

"Where are you headed?" Eve asked.

"My destination is freedom," Angie declared.

"Where's that?"

Angie smiled, "It's wherever you can find it." That smile turned into contagious laughter, and the two of them drove up the highway with the music of their laughter hugging the road.

Brian had filed a missing person's report. The police had already tapped the phone, and he waited beside it, replaying their argument over and over in his head. What did he say that could have caused such an extreme reaction? He thought that Eve had just stepped outside to clear her head. Never once did he think she wouldn't return. There was an all-points alert out on her car, and he had called every one of her friends.

By now the whole family was at the house. His mother came over to him. "Come on, son, please eat something. It'll give you strength."

His sister, Karen, complained, "This is so ridiculous. Eve is probably in some motel around the corner laughing at how hysterical we're all being. Well, I don't know about you, but I'm furious! She's going to hear from me when she walks through the door... that's a promise!"

Eve woke up alone in the car, her neck stiff from sleeping in the back seat all night. She saw Angie walking in the distance at the edge of the forest with her face tilted upward, looking at the tops of the trees. Rays of morning sun streaked between Angie's footsteps, and birds flew from tree to tree as if they were following her. Even if Eve couldn't have seen Angie she would have followed the soft jingle of the ringing bells from her bracelet. It was a subtle sound but, nonetheless, distinct enough to follow.

"What's up?" Eve asked, joining Angie.

"There's all this life around us." Angie said. "I feel so at home here."

Eve replied darkly. "I don't think I feel at home anywhere. In fact, I don't feel much of anything anymore."

"Why's that?" Angie asked, still looking upward.

"What are you looking at?" Eve questioned.

Angie replied, "Sunbeams are filtering through the trees. I can feel the energy. And the leaves crunching under our feet sound like music."

"Are you an artist or something?" Eve asked.

"No, I'm just happy to be moving through life."

Eve looked down at the moist, rich earth. "Why is it so wet here?"

"This is an Oregon rainforest," Angie said enthusiastically. "You can tell by the moss that's growing everywhere. We're bound to bump into a waterfall or two if we keep walking."

"Do you think we'll get lost?" Eve questioned.

"Well, I guess that depends on your definition of lost. By what you just said it sounds like you're already lost."

That was true. Maybe Eve could learn a thing or two from Angie. She seemed to know a lot about the forest and which berries to eat as well as which ones to stay away from. She'd say, "Watch the birds. Eat what they eat. They won't touch anything that's poisonous. You're safe with the birds."

They reached a stream, and Angie cupped her hands to drink the cool water, closing her eyes as it went down. "Mmmm, it can't get any fresher than this!" she exclaimed, grinning from ear to ear as it dripped down her chin.

Eve wondered about Angie. She seemed honest and kind, but also a bit strange. "Tell me about yourself, Angie," she asked.

"What do you want to know?"

They walked through the trees, off the beaten path, weaving around for a time, engrossed in conversation, until a flat, grassy area opened before them like a still, green lake.

They settled under a shady tree with low-slung branches. Angie climbed the nearest one and sat up high, and there she told Eve about her family and how she had always felt different and out of place growing up in New Jersey.

Angie spoke slowly, "Did you know that New Jersey has a vast forest called the Pine Barrens? No one that I've ever spoken to knows about this massive forest—in New Jersey, of all places! It was far from my house, but a boy from my school used to take me there, and he taught me a lot about nature. It was the first time I had ever been in the woods. It was like falling in love. I feel so at home surrounded by nature."

Eve was mesmerized as Angie described every scene as clearly as if it were taking place right before her eyes. "It wasn't an easy life," Angie continued. "I didn't make it an easy life. I was always running toward something I couldn't find. Searching for peace of mind. Happiness. I thought I was destined to live a lonely life. I didn't know how to fill myself—until I started listening."

"Listening to what?" Eve asked.

"Listening to me," Angie answered.

Posters with Eve's picture and vital statistics were going up all around the area. Brian did everything he could to help find her. He even went on the local television news program to make a plea.

"If anyone knows anything or has seen my wife or her car, please phone the station, and you will be generously rewarded. And if Eve is watching, please honey, come home. We're all waiting for you, and we all love you. Whatever happened, we can work it out." His eyes filled with tears, and when he finished, most of the cast and crew were openly crying.

At home, friends brought Valium, aspirin, chicken soup, Scotch and marijuana. The police stuck to the facts. Not like everyone else, with their fantasies and projections. The truth was that Brian wanted to live and die with Eve, and if something bad happened to her, then he wanted the same to happen to him.

Eve and Angie shared stories and felt as if each had experienced the same feelings at the same times in their lives. Angie sat up in that big, old tree, and they talked until the light started to fade. They laughed so hard they thought they would start crying, until Angie said, "Uh oh, the forest gets dark quickly when the sun starts going down. We'd better get back to the car."

"Gosh, I'm not even hungry. I can't believe we sat here all day!" Eve gushed.

"Yeah, me too. I guess we had a lot on our minds. Do you remember which way we entered this field?" Angie asked with a slight urgency. "Things look so different in the forest when the light changes."

"I was following you. I don't even think I looked around," Eve said casually.

Angie jumped down from the tree and began walking at a fast pace. "Okay, we'll find it. We just have to get to the main path. I didn't notice any people pass by the whole time we were talking. Did you, Eve?"

"No, not a person. You mean, you don't remember how to get back?" Eve questioned.

"Come on, let's not waste any time," Angie said, with concern in her voice.

Eve followed Angie just as she had followed her before. They walked further into the woods, and the faster they walked, the darker it got. Nothing looked familiar, and they couldn't find the main path.

Angie was out of breath and sat down on a tree stump to gather her thoughts.

"What are we going to do, Angie?" Eve asked.

Angie looked at the ground and said, "Your guess is as good as mine."

"But it seemed like you knew where you were going, like you knew your way around. I'm getting cold. Shouldn't we start screaming for help or something?" Eve urged.

"Eve, I don't want to scare you, but we're in trouble. Every forest is different, and, by the look of these trails, there are bears in this one, so I don't think we should make too much noise. We need to find shelter, and we can always pick berries and drink the water from the stream, but if there are wild dogs here, like in the Pine Barrens, we're in bigger trouble than I thought. Let's put our heads together and think of something fast, before we lose all the light."

"Put our heads together!" Eve cried. "Jesus, I'm not even comfortable at a picnic, let alone in the forest!" The look of anxiety on Angie's face added to Eve's discomfort.

"Okay," Eve said, "let's review this. We're lost in the woods. That's really all there is to say. We're lost and we're losing light, so I guess that means we're going to have to stay in the woods at least until morning, when we can see again. Right, Angie?"

"That's right, but we better find shelter fast because we need the light to see if there's any danger where we decide to spend the night."

"Danger? What kind of danger?" Eve cried.

"I mean other animals. Come on, let's move!" Angie said urgently.

They walked away from the sun so that they could take advantage of the last rays of the light. There were no caves or rocks anywhere. All they saw ahead was dense forest. Angie stopped momentarily, trying to figure the direction of a distant waterfall she thought she was hearing.

"Shh, listen, can you hear the rushing water, Eve? It's close."

Eve listened but couldn't hear what Angie heard.

Angie continued, "We must get some water so that we don't get dehydrated during the night. Follow me."

Eve followed, feeling as if this were all a dream. She was born in a big city, and was never around nature. In fact, she avoided it because it was so foreign to her. When Brian would bring up vacation ideas, he would inevitably throw in some nature trip as a joke. It was his way of teasing her, but she didn't think he fully understood the extent of her discomfort. She was praying that Angie was wrong about the bears and wild dogs, but there was also a part of her that just didn't accept that this was happening. She sensed that they would come to the main path and it would lead them to her car and they'd be off again. Off again, to where? Where was she going?

That thought was short-lived when she saw Angie stop dead in her tracks. Angie motioned for Eve to be quiet and still. Eve heard noises but couldn't quite see from where they were coming. Only the last remnants of light were in the evening sky, and Eve stood frozen with fear until she saw a little bear cub saunter up to Angie.

"Oh, look how cute!" gushed Eve as she moved toward the cub.

"Don't budge!" Angie cried.

Then, seemingly out of nowhere, with a roar that knocked Eve to the ground, a huge black bear charged at Angie. Eve turned around and started running as fast as she could while the cub playfully followed. Looking back in panic, she saw the enormous bear pulling and tugging, veering back on its hind legs and then charging again.

Eve stopped to see what the bear was doing. "This isn't happening!" she thought. She assumed that the bear hadn't seen her. She inched closer and hid behind some thick shrubs. The bear cub was preoccupied with something off to the side, and Eve was desperate to know where Angie was. She assumed that Angie had run the other way, and that they would eventually find each other.

She peeked her head up and watched the bear. It was very agitated and kept pulling on something. There was blood around its mouth and also on the ground where it stood. Eve saw the bear kicking something around, shaking its head back and forth, trying to break apart whatever it was. With one massive shake something went flying and landed about 20 feet from Eve. It was Angie's boot. When she looked back at the bear, the heart-stopping sight made her sick to her stomach and almost lose consciousness. Angie's severed foot was hanging from the bear's jaws. Eve pulled herself together and scanned the area, but she couldn't see a trace of Angie. There must be a trail of blood, but Eve couldn't see anything. She could only hear the bear's fury.

Suddenly, the bear stopped. Eve froze. It looked around, moving in her direction, grunting as it pigeon-toed its way toward her. Eve stopped breathing as it approached. Just when she thought it spotted her, the cub cried out from another direction, and, turning its huge girth, the bear lumbered off.

Eve gasped for air, and waited until she felt safe enough to move forward. She became dizzy when she passed Angie's foot lying on the ground. Half of it was chewed up, leaving only two toes. Splintered bone stuck out from the arch, and half of the heel was gone, while a large tendon hung from it like a broken rubber band. One patch of ground was blood-soaked, but that's where the trail ended. Where was Angie?

Eve didn't dare call out, but she did follow the sound of the rushing water, which was where they were headed before this happened. As Eve approached the waterfall, she heard a moaning sound from under the roaring thunder of water.

Brian was at the police station checking to see if they were still serious about searching for Eve. He thought he would go mad if he didn't hear something soon. He was convinced that this was no longer the result of their argument. He began to wonder if the police might have been right when they had suggested an illicit affair. His imagination was playing tricks on him, and his most dreaded thought was that someone had taken her or hurt her or even worse, but he couldn't let his mind go there.

Eve's picture was on every police station computer screen in the United States. Brian's plea for help on the news prompted a lot of prank calls that added to his torment. He couldn't eat. He couldn't sleep. He held onto Eve's picture as though it were glued to his hand,

and several times a minute he would look at it as if he expected it to tell him where she was.

He wasn't a religious man, but the past few days and nights he'd often close his eyes in prayer. All that he could do was wait and hold onto his sanity. It was sad and painful for his friends and family to see him this way, but they gathered around, cooking food and listening to him whenever he wanted to talk. Other than going to the police station, he wanted only to wait by the phone, from day to night, from moment to moment.

Eve found Angie behind the waterfall. Her leg was submerged in the cold water and she had tied her belt tightly around her calf to stop the bleeding. The water was tinged with red as it ran downstream. There were deep gashes on her back and sides and part of her scalp was torn off from the mauling. Barely conscious and breathing heavily, she felt that the waterfall would protect her from a return attack.

Eve didn't know the first thing about survival strategy or first aid, and Angie was losing her faculties fast. Eve filled her cupped hands with water and put them to Angie's mouth just before Angie passed out. Eve knew that she needed to get help if they were going to survive and she hoped that Angie's instinct to hide behind the water would keep her alive. After breaking some soft shrubs and placing them behind Angie's raw back, she kissed her forehead and headed into the dark forest for help.

All the light was gone now. She groped her way through the tangled forest, only stopping when she sensed danger. She lost all sense of time, and it seemed as though hours had passed. Frantic, Eve started screaming for help. She knew that she was putting her safety at risk, and picked up a heavy branch to ward off a possible attack.

Just when the pitch-black woods seemed too dense to penetrate, she suddenly broke through the trees to the flat, grassy field where she and Angie had spent the afternoon. She recognized the big tree with the low branch that Angie had sat on. The light from the moon lit up the field just enough to show the way to a thinned-out section of forest that mercifully connected with the main path that led to Eve's car. Her heart was pounding so hard that it blocked out all other sounds as she drove down the road, blasting her horn the whole way.

Angie opened her eyes and saw Eve flying over her head. It was a golden vision, but Eve didn't have any wings. "How are you doing that, Eve?" she questioned, and when she tried to move, the vision vanished. Even though the cold water had partially numbed her leg, the pain was still unbearable. Bone jutted out from where her ankle used to be, and muscle and nerve endings wiggled in the water like worms. She wasn't sure if this was a dream or reality. She called out to Eve, and when no one answered she began to shake uncontrollably and noticed her hands were turning blue.

Angie splashed her face with water and tried to use her arms to drag herself further back, but she was paralyzed by the pain. There wasn't anything that she could do but wait and try not to die. The forest sounds intensified her fear, and she vividly recalled the ferocious power that had thrown her around like a rag doll, and the sickening sound that still rang in her ears.

She almost wanted to die, to be finished with this nightmare. She closed her eyes and prayed for this to end. A strange kind of peace spread across her being, and, suddenly, she couldn't feel anything. It was as if her body had disappeared, and even though her eyes were closed she could still see where she was situated in the forest. She saw herself sitting behind the waterfall, her injured leg under the water. She even saw the bear with its cub rummaging not far in the distance.

The trees were dense, and Eve was again flying high above, without wings. Eve swooped down and cradled Angie in her arms, carrying her up over the woods toward the stars. They looked at each other without uttering a word. Finally, Eve spoke. "It is by going into the abyss that you recover the treasures of life. You must return to see the radiance everywhere." But Angie held on tight, not wanting to let go. Then Eve kissed her forehead, and Angie awoke to a roar.

She could feel the weight of the heavy paws pounding on the ground and the deafening sound was closing in. A golden light was blinding her. It was too bright. Too loud. It was tugging at her arm, trying to drag her out in the open. She wondered if it would kill her first or just rip into her belly while she was still alive. The strength overcame her. It was winning. Her leg was out of the water.

Eve was above, calling to her, reaching for her. Angie cried, "Take me! Please take me."

"We are, don't worry. You'll be alright." The man's voice had an air of authority and determination mixed with anxiety and alarm. The light from the high-beam flashlights blurred her vision. The thundering sound was from the waterfall and the people that were calling to her. Three men pulled her out and tied her to a stretcher, while Eve stood by holding Angie's hand, crying, unable to talk. When Angie saw Eve's face, she said, "Eve, are you the radiance?"

Two days and nights had passed. Eve was sitting by Angie's bedside and leaped up when she saw her eyes open. "Oh, God, Angie, you're finally awake. How do you feel?" she asked, clutching Angie's hand.

"Well, I don't really know yet. How bad was it?" Angie asked.

"Bad. It was bad," Eve replied. "They thought they were going to lose you in surgery because you had lost so much blood. While you were being operated on I gave blood for you. We have the same blood type. Imagine that."

"Did they give me your blood?" Angie asked intently.

Eve immediately responded to ease Angie's anxiety. "Yeah. They gave it to you while you were still in the operating room. It was touch and go for a while, but last night you stabilized when your fever broke. How do you feel?"

Angie was calmer now. "I feel honored that your blood is running through me. Tell me something, Eve. How did you manage to fly without wings?"

"Huh?" Eve looked confused.

"How did you fly around without wings?" Angie repeated. "You know, when you took me up in the sky and told me about the treasures of life and returning to the radiance. Are you my guardian angel?"

Puzzled and worried about Angie's mental state, Eve quietly said, "Close your eyes and rest now. I promise I'll be here when you wake up. They gave you a lot of anesthesia, so we'll talk about it when your head clears up. Okay?"

Angie became agitated, "But I have to know how you did that! Please tell me. I won't tell anyone. I swear I won't!"

Eve took Angie's hand and saw scratch marks where the bracelet with the ringing bells used to be. It must have been torn off and lost in the attack. Eve sat still while Angie dozed off, then went to the waiting room to call Brian.

Eve apologized to him for not calling sooner. Brian wanted to fly to Oregon, but she didn't want him there. She explained her ties to Angie, and the string of events that had led her there. Brian wanted to believe her story, but it was difficult to imagine, considering the intensity of the circumstances. She seemed to be recklessly blowing in the wind of indecision. She told Brian that she wasn't exactly sure when she would be coming home. That took all the air out of him.

She knew what that felt like. She knew it well. It had been three years since all the air had been taken out of Eve. She'd carried her baby for seven months, until she woke up one morning to find the sheets soaked in blood. Before she lost consciousness, she could see the baby's foot hanging out of her. Within an hour, her stillborn baby was out of her body. Eve held her dead daughter for nearly two hours, until Brian told her it was time to let go. It was at that very moment that something closed inside of her. When they came home from the hospital, Brian had already cleared out all the reminders of a newborn's arrival. There wasn't a clue. It was as if it had never happened. She knew he was trying to help. But something in her had died with her baby, and things were never the same.

Being in the hospital with Angie reignited all of those memories, and Eve didn't know what to do with her feelings. A mountain of pain and disappointment that had been building in her over the years was becoming too much for her to handle. But it was there, in front of her, and years of trying to push it away were wearing her down.

When Eve walked back to the room, Angie was trying to climb out of her bed while two nurses restrained her.

"Angie, what are you doing?" Eve shouted. "Lie down and be still."

The sound of Eve's voice calmed Angie, and when she finally settled down she started to cry. The nurses wanted to know if she was in pain, but Angie could only nod her head. Then she opened her arms to Eve, who held her quivering body until she was able to speak.

"Tell me, Eve. Please, tell me what happened. I'm so frightened and not knowing is scaring me even more. What did they do to me?" Angie begged.

Eve spoke softly. She told Angie that they had amputated her right leg above the knee and that her lung was punctured and had collapsed and that her scalp had been torn off in sections. She watched the panic in Angie's eyes turn to exhaustion. Before Angie fell asleep, Eve asked her if there was anyone that she could call, "Any family or friends? Someone?" As Angie dozed off she murmured, "No. It's just me."

One thing was for sure. If this had happened to Eve, she wouldn't be alone. The battle would still be hers, but the fighting would be easier. People who cared about her would help her. Just as they had helped when she lost the baby.

Eve stayed by Angie's side throughout every test, every pill and every doctor's opinion and diagnosis. At night, Eve slept on a couch in the waiting room and had plenty of time to think. She wanted to be free to do whatever she wanted to do, but somehow being married seemed to stop her from doing that. Or was it that she didn't really know what she wanted to do with her life, and it was easier to blame Brian and her marriage than to find the answer herself?

Eve's focus was so intense that, in order for her to gain the strength needed for this ordeal, she had to leave the hospital at times to get away. Every day she went to a park across from a nursery school and sat on a wooden bench watching the children in the playground. After the bell would ring, and everyone went back into the school building, she would look at the people in the park.

Today, in the distance, she saw a man walking toward her and watched him get larger as he came closer. It was Brian. When she recognized him her head fell into her hands and she began to cry. He sat down next to her. Silent. Afraid to say something wrong.

Eve finally spoke. "Why did you come here, Brian?"

"I came because I love you," he said quietly.

"But I told you not to come," she said angrily.

"I couldn't stand being away from you another night."

Eve's voice softened as she whimpered, "I'm so sorry, Brian."

"Eve, do you have any idea what you've put me and the family through by not contacting us?" His demeanor was calm.

"It's actually taken this long for me to fathom all that has happened," she answered.

Brian continued. "I don't even know how to respond to all of this. Why are you staying here, in Oregon, with someone you hardly know?"

Eve knew that he was trying to be accepting, but he couldn't really understand because she needed to sort it out first.

"How did you know I'd be here?" she asked.

"The hospital told me. And I thought you'd be watching children."

Eve looked at him. "Brian, I've committed to help Angie, and I can't give you a straight answer because I can't even guess how long it will take. It's been a long time since I've had the feeling of being needed, of having a purpose in life. Do you even understand a little of what I'm saying? I'm not blaming you," she continued. "I know that you always want what's best for me."

"I don't know," he said. "I'm not sure I know who you are anymore."

"*I'm* not even sure who I am anymore!" Eve cried. "But I do know that for me to be happy it has to come from inside myself. After all that's happened, I have to find out who I've become."

That was exactly what all of this was about. "I need time to figure things out. For the past few years I've been avoiding myself by being what you and everyone else wanted me to be. I got lost in the shuffle." She wondered if Brian could really understand what she was saying. "I know that changes have to take place in order for me to move on. I just don't know what they are. But I do know that I just can't do it this way anymore."

Eve knew her only chance at living the life she wanted for herself was to be brave enough to follow her heart. It was that simple. That hard. She loved Brian, and he loved her, but she didn't want to be disconnected from life anymore.

When they got back to the hospital room, Angie's bed was empty, and her wheelchair was gone. The head nurse came in and asked if Angie was with her.

"What do you mean? Where is she?" Eve responded.

"We don't know!" the nurse cried. "There was an emergency on the floor, and when everything settled down we checked on her and she was gone. Since you were also gone we thought that you might have taken her somewhere."

"What are you talking about?" Eve shouted. "Where would I take her?"

"I'd better tell the supervisor that she isn't with you." Then, the nurse stopped and turned back to Eve, pulling a note from her pocket. "Oh, I almost forget, this was on the bed when we discovered that she was gone. Maybe you'll understand it. We didn't."

Brian interrupted, "What's happening, Eve?"

Eve's hands were shaking as she read the words boldly written on the torn white paper. "It is by going into the abyss that you recover the treasures of life. You must return to see the radiance everywhere."

After the hospital was searched, Eve and Brian drove all around looking for Angie, then went back to the hospital and waited for another three hours. Brian never left her side. Eve kept reading the note. They got back in the car and searched one more time. Since Angie didn't know Eve's last name, or where she lived, Eve left her home phone number for Angie at the nurses station.

Brian drove down the coast. It started raining when they were passing the section of highway where Eve had met Angie. "Brian, pull over please. I just want to be here for a moment." The big pines were silhouetted in front of the endless, moonlit sky. Eve told Brian how Angie had looked the night that she approached the car, and how dramatically both of their lives had changed since then. She relived the whole story. Suddenly, she wondered if it had all been a dream. Had she hit her head harder than she thought? Was it all some strange hallucination?

Not far from them, they saw a deer walking slowly across the road. Eve sat motionless. Everything was quiet except for the familiar sound of gentle ringing bells. Standing before her, washed in the luminous, golden glow from the headlights, stood the deer. It was looking directly at her. The large eyes seemed to speak to her. Eve didn't move. She didn't even breathe. She sat still, hypnotized by the sight.

High on the mighty antlers was a silver bracelet with two little bells that rang softly as the deer moved away. "Wait!" Eve cried. Jumping out of the car she faced this messenger. For one last moment the deer remained, and then it vanished into the black night.

Eve watched it disappear behind the trees. She had seen the radiance. The light that had been there all along, but was too bright to see, was now lighting her way. She had found her peace. And she knew the sound of the ringing bells would stay with her forever.

In the cemetery, I told my brother to walk on the path that was six graves to the left while I took the one on the right. We kept yelling to each other to see if either of us had found our maternal grandparents. Suddenly, my brother called, "I think this is it." I walked to where he was standing and stopped in front of five graves bunched together. The grave of my mother's father was lying next to two tall tombstones. His oval picture was on his stone, and my grandmother's picture was diagonally behind him. All my life I had seen these pictures hanging on the walls of our various apartments, never knowing that these were their eternal images left behind.

The two graves next to my grandfather were of his parents. My great grandparents. My brother and I had never even known that they had made it to the United States. The grave next to my grandmother was my grandfather's sister, our great aunt, whom we had also never heard of. I wanted so deeply to feel affection for these five relatives. The bones of my ancestors were buried in front of me in this obscure Jewish Orthodox Cemetery where no one ever came to visit. These were the graves of forgotten families.

I wanted to feel forgiveness, like I did for my paternal grandfather, but this side of the family was different. This was where my mother came from. She never liked her father much, and spoke of him as though he were a womanizer. He married a few times after my grandmother died. My mother never approved of his other marriages. All that I remember of my grandfather is that he gave me gum and a nickel when I sat on his lap. I was four years old when he died. He was the only living grandparent that I had.

But I couldn't stop wondering about the three nearby graves. Why had I never heard of these people? Where had they lived? What did they do? I knew that most of my grandmother's family had been killed, in Poland, first by the Cossacks and then, ultimately, in concentration camps. But it seemed my grandfather's timing was fortunate enough that he was able to bring his family to America, keeping them as safe as they could be, given the circumstances. Perhaps that's why I was never told. Maybe the stories were too frightening for a young child to hear.

THE CLEANING LADY

She took big gulps from the honey-colored bottle of Jack Daniels that was sitting on the floor beside her. The office was lit solely by the evening skyline glow from outside the open window. She felt safe on the 12th floor of this old Chicago building. She knew the only way to survive a fall from that height was if this were all just a dream, and if it were, she would simply spread her outstretched arms and fly away.

The lampshade near her face tilted like an old lady's hat in the wind. She had knocked it over and was already too drunk to fix it, or to finish the suicide note that was threatening to blow off her desk from the night breeze. But her mind was still clear enough not to make any sudden moves toward the open window.

The shadows in the room aged her face, etching deep lines around her mouth and her expressionless eyes. She stared at the white wall nearest her as if watching a silent movie. She was pretty in an elusive way, mysterious in her shroud of secrecy. Her lips parted slightly as if stopped in mid sentence, and her dress seductively rode up her long legs, but there was no heat coming from her body. Her dark hair waved in sections, but was stringy in others, as though she had twisted and pulled the curl from it with her long, desperate fingers.

She was surprised to hear a noise that sounded as if it were coming from the outside hall. No one worked late on this floor, she was sure of that. These last few weeks she had double checked locations, and this office was definitely the most isolated one. Then what was that rumble? And that voice?

"Hello? Excuse me, is someone in here? I can come back later to straighten up if you'd like. Hello? I'll just close the window. Your papers are flying off your desk, and, oh goodness, I think the wind pushed your lamp over!"

The cleaning lady walked into the broken light of the room. Her graying hair still had some brown remnants of her youth, and her skin was translucent, as if you could see the blood rushing underneath. Her posture bent forward as though she were carrying a sizable weight on her shoulders, making her small frame appear even more fragile.

As she approached the desk she saw the woman sitting on the floor. Her voice was strong with a slight European accent.

"Oh, excuse me! Wh-what are you doing on the floor, Miss? Did you fall? Are you all right?"

The woman slid closer to the cabinet and mumbled in a low voice, "Please, just go away, I'm fine."

The cleaning lady registered little surprise as she spoke to the woman. "I don't know what's troubling you, but maybe you should go home, if you don't mind me saying so?"

The woman lashed out, "Well I *do*! Come back tomorrow and the office will be empty. I guarantee it."

The cleaning lady leaned in closer. "I think you've had a little too much to drink for your own good. Can I call a cab for you? Or do you have a husband or any relatives that live around here?"

The woman had a faraway look in her eyes. Her voice was faint. "I have a brother." Grabbing at the paper on the desk, the cleaning lady responded, "Here then, give me his number and I'll call him for you."

The woman ignored her. "My brother's always there when I need him."

As the woman spoke, the cleaning lady read the sheet of paper she had taken from the woman's desk, and as she read the blood drained from her cheeks. She stood silently watching the woman pour another drink. Then she walked to the window and closed it.

The woman tried to stand but lost her balance. "Don't do that!" she shouted. "No one said you could close the window! I want it open. Open it!"

The cleaning lady opened the window and pushed her cart out of the way so that she could sit near the woman. They sat looking at each other for a few minutes, and then she asked, "Is your brother younger or older than you?"

"Four years older," she answered.

"Oh, that's nice. A big brother. I'll bet he used to stick up for you when you were children... Yes?"

"I guess."

"Tell me about him." The cleaning lady tried to engage the woman. "I never had a brother. I'm curious to know."

They sat in the stillness. The woman's eyelids were getting heavy, and she laughed a little to herself. "When I was a kid I wanted to be like my brother. I used to bend my knees way forward when I walked." The woman's eyes clouded over as though she were talking to herself. The cleaning lady sat on the floor and listened.

"I slept in the dining room 'til I was 14 years old. For years I used to think a little man was going to come out of the kitchen and stab me in the neck. Even in the heat of summer I would wrap a big blanket around my neck before I went to sleep. I hated my brother then, for a lot of reasons, but mainly because he had the other bedroom. Then, he joined the Air Force. When he left I actually prayed for a war so that he'd be killed, and I would finally have the bedroom all to myself."

The cleaning lady smiled. The woman smiled back. "I painted it pink and black."

"And your brother?"

"He changed. He wrote me long letters about how we had the same blood and that nothing could ever change that. It was strange because he never wanted to be with me before. But now he wanted me to trust him."

The cleaning lady shivered and wrapped her arms around her torso to hold onto her own heat. "Yes, I know about that. Many people don't trust me. They think because I clean up after them that I'll steal something or snoop around."

The woman turned her head away, and the cleaning lady immediately asked another question. "What happened to your brother?"

"I wrote to him about the problems I had at home. He sent me the most wonderful letters about courage and honesty. They were poetic. He didn't blame me or make me feel guilty. I remember thinking he really understood me, and that I wasn't as alone as I thought." She looked up at the cleaning lady. "You want a drink?"

The cleaning lady uneasily shifted her weight back and forth. "I could call him for you. The phone is right here on the desk."

The woman answered sharply, "No. Whatever I decide will come from *me!*"

The cleaning lady wanted to call for help but was too afraid to leave the woman alone. "Do you live around here?"

"Have you noticed the little old man who walks around the neighborhood? I think he had a stroke and his daughter's always screaming at him to hurry up. I haven't seen him for a while. He takes tiny steps, and his hands and head shake uncontrollably. He looks so old with his drippy eyes. I'm not sure if it's from the stroke or if he's crying. Have you seen him lately? I wonder if he died."

The woman's voice sounded far away. "I can see him so clearly. His black coat and his scuffed shoes. His trembling hands. I even see the cracks in the sidewalk where he takes his tiny steps. He's in my memory, and I've never spoken one word to him."

The woman's face hung down so low that her chin rubbed against her chest. Her body looked broken, and she was crying. The cleaning lady could barely understand her. She brought out a box of tissues from her cart and put her hand on the woman's shoulder.

When the woman calmed down, the cleaning lady pleaded, "How about if I call your brother just to tell him you're here, please?"

"No."

"Are you cold?"

"No."

"I'm freezing."

"So go."

"Where is your brother?"

"He came back home when he finished the Air Force. From that point on we were constantly together. We'd take long rides to the wealthy North Side neighborhoods, and we'd look at those big, expensive homes and dream about what it would be like to live inside one of them."

The cleaning lady listened anxiously as the woman continued. "In winter, ivy veins wound around the old campus buildings at Northwestern, and we watched the blond, red-cheeked students in their plaid and corduroy clothes. One time we stopped for lunch at a coffee shop around there and when we were leaving a guy looked at me and asked, 'Are you Jewish?' I said, 'Are you kidding?' My brother took me by the arm and we left, and from then on that neighborhood never really felt the same to me."

The cleaning lady's face was very still and her eyes were glassy as she sat motionless on the floor. It looked as if she were looking through the woman. In a distant voice she said, "Yes, I know that feeling."

The woman's eyes momentarily cleared and she asked sharply, "How do you know?"

The cleaning lady looked confused. "Excuse me?"

The woman answered, forming her words slowly and carefully, "You just said that you knew what I meant. You said, 'I know that feeling.' What did you mean?" The woman seemed defensive. There was a slight fear that was hidden in the cleaning lady's eyes. She spoke quietly. "You've been drinking a lot. Wouldn't you like to go home to your nice warm bed and wake up to a new day? Aren't you getting tired?"

The woman repeated emphatically, "*How do you know?*"

The cleaning lady fidgeted with her hands, and didn't seem quite sure of how to handle this question. She was there to help this woman, and she decided to confront her with blunt honesty. "I know what you're trying to do. I read your letter and I see that you're in pain. But I think you just need time and a clear mind and to be with people that care about you."

The woman's eyes rolled up as she laughed sarcastically and said, "Yeah, sure, people that care about me, that's just what I need! Don't you know that when you need people the most, they're not there? Where were they for little Gary?"

"Who's that?"

"This five-year-old kid who used to run around the streets. He was always filthy."

"What happened to him?" The cleaning lady asked.

"It was the first day of school after summer vacation. It looked like an ordinary day, but there was a kind of emptiness in the air. When I got home my mom told me that something terrible had happened. The little boy who used to play in the alley ran in front of a truck and was killed."

The woman continued nervously as a thin film glazed over her eyes. "I ran down the back porch steps and stopped when I saw a shimmering red puddle at the end of the alley. The reflection of the sun made it sparkle but it was so still. It was all that was left of Gary. A red puddle. I'll bet if you put a drop under a microscope you could still see his life moving around, but he would never move again."

"There was a high-pitched ring in the air. Like when I was a kid and just before my appendix operation they put a mask, soaked with ether, on my face. The doctor told me to watch the second hand on the Mickey Mouse clock, and I heard this high-pitched ring, and it echoed, and it felt like time was suspended. Everything stopped except the high-pitched ring... I've been hearing it a lot lately."

"Please, Miss," the cleaning lady pleaded, "let's call your brother now. Don't you want to talk to him?"

The woman was looking at the cleaning lady's hair. "Did you know that when you're a beautician, people talk to you like you're a psychiatrist or something? During my final month of beauty school I was putting curlers in this woman's hair. She was my last customer, and I wanted to go home. I hadn't been listening to her. Then, I heard her say that she had a few months left to live. I focused on this woman's face in the mirror. She told me that the Mayo Clinic had told her that she had thyroid cancer, and that's why her eyes bugged out of her head.

"I started to hear that high-pitched ring. I went to my supervisor and asked her to finish my customer. I told her I was leaving. She followed me to my locker and asked where I was going. I said I was quitting. She saw that I was upset, and I told her that the lady was dying and that I didn't want to be a beautician anymore.

"I called my brother to pick me up, and we drove to the North Side and he tried to comfort me. I didn't know what to be now that I had quit beauty school. The more he talked, the quieter the ring got. Until he made me laugh. Then it disappeared."

The cleaning lady interrupted, "I know that high-pitched ring. I heard it when I was a young girl in school, just around the time the fighting started..."

The cleaning lady saw a slight smile on the woman's face and asked, "Are you hungry?"

"No."

It was suddenly very quiet in the room. The cleaning lady broke the silence with another question. "Does your brother live around here?"

"I know what you're trying to do," the woman said. "You're getting me to talk about my past. Getting me all worked up and sentimental to take my mind off of why I originally decided to kill myself." The tone in her voice accelerated, "Look, you don't have to do this. In fact, I don't really want you here. You don't even know me! All you want to do is talk me out of this so you can take all the credit for saving someone's life. Then you can get on the news or win something, so all your friends and family will give you a big party, and you'll have this moment to put in your scrapbook."

"I don't have a family," the cleaning lady said softly.

"Well, I'm sorry about that, but did you ever think that maybe I don't want to see another sunset? Maybe I'm just sick of breathing! Maybe I have an incurable disease or maybe my whole family was wiped out by some sniper on top of a bank building. So don't go pushing all of your, 'Isn't life wonderful,' bullshit in my face. You don't know me at all."

The cleaning lady moved to the open window and looked down as the breeze blew her hair away from her face, "We all hurt," she said under her breath. For a moment she looked as if she were going to lean over and just drop out of sight.

The scene frightened the woman, and she shouted, "Stop! What are you doing?" The woman was shocked and angered, "What are you trying to prove? You're just trying to scare me. I'm not falling for this..."

The cleaning lady stood still, never turning to look at the woman's face. "I heard what you were telling me about your life. I even felt sorry for you."

The woman sat pale and frozen on the floor, and when she attempted to stand her knees refused to lift her. Her voice was shaky. "How can you say that?" she said. "We've only spent a little time together. I never even told you why I'm here." Then, she threw her hands up in the air and laughed. "You're a cleaning lady! I'm listening to a cleaning lady!"

The cleaning lady ironically laughed with her, "Yes, you're listening to a cleaning lady. I clean up other people's lives because it's too late to clean up my own. I have no brother and no family, but I do have a number I can't wash off my arm."

The cleaning lady spoke softly, "I was only nine years old when they brought us to the camp. My sister and I were so frightened when they separated us from our mother and father. As they marched us away we cried and kept turning around to see where they were taking our parents. This one guard kept telling me I was going to burn up and die, always smiling as he talked of these horrors. It looked like such a friendly smile, but what he said made me cry even harder. The cement floor that I slept on made my bones feel like they were made of ice. One night I just couldn't stop crying. The smiling guard came by and said, 'Oh, you miss your mother? Poor child, come with me.' His smile always confused me because his words were so frightening."

"He took me down a long corridor into a large, empty room with water faucets on the walls. There were drains all over the floor. He told me to stand against the farthest wall and wait there and he would bring my mother to me. He was smiling."

The woman rocked back and forth on the floor. "You don't have to tell me this story, really."

The cleaning lady gave no response, "I waited for hours, and then the door swung open, and my mother was standing in the doorway. She looked so tired and her hair was all matted down. When she saw me, she opened her arms, and I ran to her from across the large empty room. As I got closer, I saw the guard standing behind my mother. He was smiling at me, and because he had helped me, I smiled back. Then he grabbed my mother from behind and slit her throat from ear to ear. Just as I reached her, her body fell to the floor and I saw the light leave her eyes. The guard said, 'Now you have something to cry about!' Her blood was running down the drains in the floor and was dripping off his knife as he came at me. But someone entered the room and saw my mother lying there and started to yell at him. I never cried again. I had killed my mother with my tears, and was afraid they would do the same to my father or sister if I cried again."

The woman sat motionless, except for the tears that slid down her cheeks. The cleaning lady kneeled next to her. After a few moments, in a weak voice, the woman said, "I think I want to call my brother."

The cleaning lady held out her hand to help her up. The woman was unsteady but somehow felt stronger. They walked to the window and the cleaning lady closed it with one hand while her other arm held on to the woman. They looked at each other without speaking. The woman stared deep into the cleaning lady's eyes until she saw her own reflection. It was a kind face that she saw. Maybe a little more frightened than it should be, but it was a face that had life inside of it. She wondered if they were alike but then dismissed the thought. She was tired. Too tired to notice the cleaning lady gently nudging her away from the once-opened window.

We sat in silence as we drove from the cemetery. The blood of those souls runs through us. To deny them is to deny ourselves. The farther we drove the more I couldn't stop reflecting on that remote cemetery. I wanted so much to feel for those lost relatives. But I was numb. I am somewhat closed to my mother, and maybe that was the numbness I felt. Maybe I have no feeling. Or maybe I feel too much. It was easier with my paternal grandfather because my heart is more open to my father.

Suddenly, I had the urge to revisit my own roots. "Lets go to the old neighborhood," I said. The look in my brother's eyes made me sad. Even though he lived in Chicago, it was hard for him to relive these deep memories and the feelings they stirred up. He never thought about the past, or so he said. He wasn't steeped in the nostalgia that I felt each time my feet touched Chicago ground. It was day-to-day life for him and he never went to the old neighborhood.

When I would come to visit we'd usually drive down Sheridan Road and wind our way north to the wealthy areas to see the stoic mansions that lined Lake Michigan with guest houses, private beaches and gazebo-spotted landscapes. We'd pass the scream of color that floods the eyes in autumn or winter's constant skeletal backdrop.

But I loved my neighborhood. The streets and alleys were home to me. I would pick lilacs from the bushes in the alley, and ride my racer on the side streets as if I owned them. My close friends comforted and accepted me, put up with my vivid imagination and fantasy life. Sometimes my imagination worked for me and sometimes it worked against me… but it was always working.

CURIOSITY

There is a place of total peace somewhere. I know it like I know the palm of my hand. If I closed my eyes I would see my hand clearly in my mind, but the details would escape me. The branches of my lifeline, the rivers that break from the furrows where it bends would elude me, as if remembering someone's forehead or chin that you haven't seen in a long time.

I know the feeling of peace. It is familiar, but from where I know it I don't remember. Maybe it was as a sleeping baby or maybe before I was a baby. That before-birth place. All those sperm swimming around in testicles, or those timely eggs. All those possibilities landing in a puddle on someone's white linen sheet, or washed away in a pool of monthly blood.

There are living angels walking among us. Maybe we're all angels of a sort, but some reveal themselves more clearly. Their hope and innocence outshine the vast darkness. But if a cataclysmic event of such proportion as to threaten the entire life force were to happen, I believe that angels would appear in abundance. Human goodness would flood the moral blindness of greed and power. There would be no need for those merciless ways. Or maybe not.

I am walking down the street with these thoughts flashing through my mind when I see, from behind, a strange creature walking ahead of me. I question its femininity even though it is dressed like a woman. My curiosity gets the best of me, and I follow whatever it is into a hotel lobby coffee shop. I sit down in full view of—I'm still unsure of what to call it—and watch for a while. I think it's a she, but the jaw line is somewhat masculine, and there is so much face powder caked on the skin that I'm suspicious of a beard.

Other than that and a lean, rather shapeless figure, it's really quite beautiful. I'm not using "it" in a demeaning or derogatory manner, mind you, I'm just unsure how to identify this rather spectacular he/she. Its long black hair falls gracefully onto bone-white shoulders, and its deep blue eyes, the color of the open ocean, watch the passersby from the restaurant window. I watch it watching. We are the only patrons of this establishment, save the waiters and busboys who pay no attention, whatsoever, to this inexplicable beauty.

Large hands. It has large hands. I'm still uncertain. It sips iced tea from a straw as lazily as the moisture that slides down the sides of the tall glass. I am mesmerized by this vision. Clothing is a burden as heat emanates in waves from the ground on this humid, scorching summer day. It's wearing one of those sarong-type skirts with a slit up the front, and I can see the skin between its thighs, momentarily, stick together when it uncrosses its legs. A gauzy, sleeveless blouse reveals small breasts covered by a lacy camisole.

Leaving the glass half empty and some coins on the table it glides out. Intrigued, I follow it to the hotel's front desk, where it picks up a room key and enters the elevator. I wait, sitting on a couch in the lobby, and 20 minutes later it emerges, wearing a short robe that covers a black bathing suit. The pool is in the back, and I walk slowly behind hypnotically following. It stops at a green lounge chair and with its back to me, drops its robe to the hot pavement.

Its body is rather straight with no real indentation at the waist. The brief, two-piece bathing suit reveals little, although there is little to reveal. It turns around and I see a slight cleavage, a flat belly and smooth crotch—but when one is steeped in deceit it is easy to deceive.

I sit in the shade at a round table with a large umbrella overhead. My dark sunglasses hide the curiosity in my eyes, and I hold a newspaper, casually left on a nearby chair, in front of my face. It takes its time rubbing suntan lotion almost adoringly on its smooth skin. Its hand slowly wipes tiny drops of oil up one soft leg and onto the other. In a single, graceful motion it dives into the blue, chlorinated water, cutting through the inconspicuous liquid for two full lengths. It surfaces, face first, lifting its body from the deep end exposing defined muscles from each side of its thin arms. It makes me wonder.

The hot sun evaporates beads of water that dot its skin. I can almost see a halo of steam rising from its body as it lies on the lounge with its eyes closed. Motionless, like a desert sphinx, in the bright afternoon sun. Its tongue moistens its lips from one corner to the other. I sit still, but my heart quickens and I am oddly out of breath.

It gets up, puts the robe on and begins to leave. Hesitating after a few steps, it turns around and walks to the far end of the pool. A curious move since there is no exit from there. Turning left at one corner then walking to the other it drags my eyes wherever it goes. With one last turn it approaches and passes right before me, as if in slow motion, and I watch until it disappears into the elevator.

I am sweating, but the heat I feel has nothing to do with the summer sun. As I stand to reach in my pocket for my handkerchief, my hand strikes something on the table in front of me. I am momentarily blinded by the sun's reflection on a shiny object. It is a hotel key to room 512. I vaguely remember hearing a sound as it passed by but couldn't pull myself away from watching. Without even looking it had placed the key in front of me. This was a deliberate and reckless invitation.

My hand trembles as I wipe my brow, and, grappling with the key, I somewhat stumble to the elevator and press the fifth-floor button. Blood courses through my body at such a speed it sounds like the roar of a lion. A roar of battle, power and territory. Hunting and stalking. But was I stalking or was I being stalked?

I walk down the dimly lit corridor and stand in front of the closed door. I slip the key in the keyhole, but decide to knock instead of entering. The door opens. We stand there, wondering. It moves to the side to let me in. The room is small and I sit on the end of the bed. It sits across from me on a chair near the television. We look at each other. Silent and still.

"You're confused," it finally says. "You don't know if I'm a man or a woman, do you?"

I watch and listen to its deep, but feminine voice. As it speaks, its mouth moves as if it were tasting something sweet and delicious, but it is difficult for me to watch and listen at the same time.

It continues, "I know that I've caught you off guard. I imagine I am a bit of a threat and strange to you. Which am I? How do you find me?"

I'm not even sure that an audible sound will come forth, but I answer quietly. "I find you irresistible," I utter.

A slight smile colors its face. "Then what difference does it matter what I am?" It continues speaking as it approaches me. "If I am irresistible, and you can have me, then why not take me? I wouldn't be in this situation if I weren't curious myself. I saw you watching me from the very beginning."

It takes the sunglasses from my face and says, "I could feel your eyes burning through me at the pool."

It kneels in front of me sliding my jacket off my shoulders, trapping my arms. Its face is inches from mine when it loosens my collar. After pushing me back on the bed it takes my shoes off and runs both its hands up my trouser legs stopping only inches from my crotch. Then, it stands and unbuttons its long, silky dress, exposing a black, fitted body suit underneath, covering its mystery.

Its long legs pour over the lower half of my body and I release my arms and wrap them around its torso. It supports the upper half of its body with each hand on the side of my shoulders. Covering me in one slow motion, I inhale the scent of sweet lilies from its long dark hair falling over my face. We turn our bodies around and I look down on this intoxicating sexual puzzle. I hold its face in my hands feeling its smooth cheek then lower myself until we kiss. Its kiss is more aggressive than mine, darting its tongue in and out of my mouth in an impersonal, pornographic way. We seem out of sync.

It wants me to undress and asks if I have any protection. "Yes," I say, but I want to take my time and I slide my hand up the side of its body feeling its small, firm breasts. Its body is muscular within its small frame. Hard legs. Tight stomach. When I move my hand up the inside of its thigh it stops me and whispers, "Not yet. Let me go first."

It gets up, unzips my pants and pulls them off. On top of me again it kisses my neck, and while one hand is pulling at my shirt the other goes between my legs. It takes a moment for it to realize that I'm not what it thought I was. It isn't used to the wet fire that beckons the hardness of a man. When its eyes open and it sees my soft breasts exposed from under my shirt, it whispers, "Oh, no!" I knew it was only a matter of time before those words would have come from either one of us, only this time the battle was mine to win.

On hot summer nights, my father and I would sit on the back porch and look up at the stars through the telephone wires that lined the alley. He would talk about gravity and time and space, and tell me that the twinkling star I was looking at may no longer be there. I might just be seeing its light that had died long ago, and time hadn't caught up with it yet. He knew how to simplify subjects that I thought were far too complicated, but after his explanations I understood them perfectly.

I'd come home in the late afternoon and my father would usually be asleep in the living room chair after an exhausting day of work. The newspaper would be on his lap while a backdrop of classical music played softly. Sometimes, if he were awake, he'd tell me stories that he imagined the music was suggesting. In my mind I'd vividly see every scene that he described. Between the music and the drama in his voice I would become so emotional that I'd inevitably begin to cry.

He was a good storyteller and had great humor. Yet as quick as my father was to laugh, he was quick to yell. There were nightly arguments that were so loud that the neighbors would hit the walls and ceilings with a broom to tone down the decibel level coming from our apartment. I would hold my ears to cushion the sound. But my father's imagination frightened me more than his yelling, and he used it often. He didn't understand that I was too young and impressionable to hear the dark creations of an adult mind.

My mother was predictably unpredictable. Troubled in many ways. Yet she had the excitement of a child and was always young at heart. And her laugh was like fluttering bright ribbons that could momentarily fill our drab apartment with color. But the times were against her, and she couldn't get the medical help she needed. She would have been happier if she had gotten the right treatment. But she was lost inside a troubled mind, and no one understood how to help her or how much help she really needed.

I am from my parents, and not to love them would mean that I don't love all of who I am, because they are a part of the whole of who I am. How could I ever forgive myself if I never forgave them? My memories were suddenly full of sadness and pain for all the mistakes that were made. Shame on me, and shame on them, and shame on their parents, and theirs, and theirs. I was willing to do anything to break this cycle.

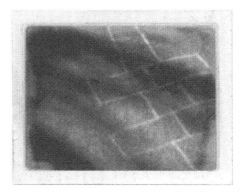

CONFRONTATION

Grace spoke out loud to the imaginary little girl sitting next to her in the car. "I'm going to take care of you. Don't worry. I won't let anything bad happen to you. I promise." She looked at the empty seat, but in her mind she saw two brown eyes, filled with fear, staring back at her, and little girl legs so small they couldn't even bend with the curvature of the seat.

She couldn't really focus on all of the details that she wanted to discuss with her parents. Discuss was the correct word. She didn't want to get angry. She didn't want to be specific. All she wanted to talk about was what happened in the past that was stopping her from living her life now. She had tried different types of psychotherapy, biofeedback, medical doctors, holistic practitioners, self-help programs. She even burned letters on the beach to release the negative feelings she held inside since childhood, but to no avail.

She had just spent three months in and out of the hospital with an immobilizing pain in the right lower side of her belly. The pain-management specialist suggested that it could be from internalized anger. "Could even be from childhood," he said.

Finally they discovered it was a cyst inside of her spinal canal, referring the pain to her belly. It was treated, and that was behind her now, but what he had said about how damaging it was to hold onto internalized pain still rang true to her. Now Grace was attempting to save herself by having a confrontation with her parents. As far as she was concerned, this was her last resort.

She didn't want to wait for her parents to die so that she could visit their graves to tell them what she needed to say now. Grace was attempting to make room for the possibility of their having better times together once she released the anger. As it was now, simply the sound of her mother's voice sent a disturbing feeling through her body, and even her father's once-perfect behavior was, now, full of faults. She called less, and rarely wanted to see them. The worst part was the guilt she felt. The guilt of not being a good daughter. Of harboring such dark feelings for the people who gave her life. She prayed this visit would help rid her of it. She prayed for guidance and strength.

After pulling into her parents' driveway, she turned off the ignition and took the imaginary little girl's hand. "Don't be afraid," she said, "I promise I will take care of you. No one will hurt you." Standing at their front door, holding onto the tiny, invisible hand, her heart was pounding while her mind desperately searched for the right words. The door opened and her father, Paul, stood behind the screen smiling as he greeted her. She had called earlier in the week to set up this meeting. Her mother, Lillie, walked into the room with the troubled look of anticipation on her face. She hadn't been feeling well and wanted to postpone this visit but, sensing the urgency, she hesitantly agreed.

Paul and Lillie sat close together on one couch as Grace sat on the other, carefully placing the little girl to her left, winking at her before beginning.

"This isn't going to be easy for me to say, and I know it isn't going to be easy for you to hear. But I have done everything in my power to avoid this day, and I don't know what else I can do. This seems to be my last recourse." Her parents looked concerned.

Grace took a deep breath and alternated between looking at the carpet and their faces as she spoke. "There are things that have happened to me in my childhood that have, in many ways, stopped my life. I've carried those things inside of me for so long, and now it's time to give them to you to carry." She looked directly at them. "By the way, please don't interrupt me. I just want to say what I came here to say."

Lillie interrupted. "What is it?"

"I'm trying. It isn't easy," Grace calmly continued. "I've lived my whole life trying to get you both to accept me. I'm sick of trying. I have to say that most of what I'm about to say is directed toward you, Mom, although I do have some issues with you, Dad. But it's mostly Mom. And no one has put me up to this. My therapist even told me I shouldn't do this because it wouldn't make any difference. But I had to. I didn't want to wait for both of you to die and then go to your graves to tell you. I'm doing this to free myself of the burden that has weighed upon me."

Lillie interrupted again. "I don't know. When I was a child, my mother..."

Grace stopped her in mid-sentence. "I am not here to talk about you, Mom. I'm here to talk about me. Now allow me to struggle through this, please."

Paul stopped Lillie from talking, and they both looked wide-eyed with anticipation as Grace gathered her thoughts and turned to her mother. Her lower jaw was quivering from fear as she spoke. "I don't want to take care of you anymore, Mom. Your problems are your own, and it drains me to hear your constant complaining. I try to solve your problems for you and none of my solutions are considered and you continue complaining. I was a sweet, sensitive little girl, and you mistreated me. I never deserved it. I virtually raised myself to stay out of your way."

From the corner of her eye she could see a little foot reaching for the floor as if to run away but it just dangled in midair, waiting. Grace continued. "My life is about fear and anxiety, and that came directly from both of you. I was emotionally abandoned by you, and now when I'm with you it doesn't feel good."

Grace turned her attention to her father. "And, Dad, your greatest sin was not rescuing me from Mom's insanity. You had all the right words, and it was confusing because I believed you. I believed your drama, but it was all a smoke screen that I couldn't depend on."

Paul and Lillie listened to their only daughter speak a parents' nightmare. Lillie interrupted again. "You know, I don't even remember the things that happened back then. My mother treated me badly, but I loved her so much, and to this day I dream..."

Grace talked over her mother's words in a firm and gentle tone. "I am not here to talk about you, Mom. I know about you. I want you to know about me. You were cruel to me for no reason when I was a child, and because of that it's hard for me to feel loving feelings toward you."

"Like what? What did I do, hit you? Every parent hits their children!"

"I never hit my daughter, and anyway, that's not the point." Grace stared at the carpet thinking of how to get back on track. Paul stopped his wife. "Let her speak."

Grace continued with more agitation in her voice. "You're obsessed with yourself, Mom. You want me to take care of you, and I don't want that job anymore. I never did! I quit!"

Now Lillie talked right over Grace. "My mother would hit me, and she never told me that she loved me. But I always knew she loved me."

"Mom, I've heard these stories all my life. I've been overlooked and ignored by both of you because of your self-obsession. I've tried to have a relationship with you, but it's an unrealistic expectation, and I give up. I want you to know that I'm giving up. I don't want the responsibility anymore. It's too much work. It's too hard. And it's destroying me. I must take care of myself now."

During this entire time, what surprised her most was the sense of calm that was centered in her storm. Paul and Lillie sat on the couch and listened to her every word. Grace turned to the little girl. Her young, innocent eyes looked less afraid.

"I'm plagued by insecurities and fear," Grace confessed. "Governed by them. They have gotten in my way all of my life, and they're from you. And now I'm giving them back to you."

Lillie got up and sat on a couch across the room, facing Grace, and began to speak. "When I was a little girl, my mother..."

"Mom!" she shouted, "Stop talking about yourself!" Grace stood up and yelled, "I'm your daughter! I'm telling you terrible things about how I feel about you! What are you feeling about all of this? This isn't about you and your mother, it's about us! Don't you have any feelings at all about what I've been saying?"

Lillie sat on the couch wringing her skinny hands. Her hazel eyes were wide and reddening as she responded. "Well, I feel awful. I think what you're saying is horrible. I—I feel—mortified!"

She watched her mother continue speaking from across the room, but she didn't hear the words. Grace could only see a wounded, fragile soul sitting there. Someone who was in unknown territory.

She was suddenly touched by her mother's feelings. No rage. No anger. Grace was really seeing her mother. There was light in this moment, and it was far more than she could have ever hoped for. She knew that this was just a beginning, but she was grateful for the relief.

As Grace walked slowly toward her mother, her heart opened with each step and she kneeled and embraced her.

Even though Grace was afraid, and her mother looked mortified, they both opened to each other as she sobbed in her mother's arms. She was being comforted, and she knew that it was coming from deep within her.

Lillie murmured, "Don't worry, it's all right. Come on now." But these tears needed release. She could hear her father crying from the other couch. She had come home and was being nurtured and cared for at that moment, and that moment was all she could have asked for.

Maybe this experience had made room to explore the good things she had learned from them, but she couldn't think of that now. Grace lifted herself up and knew that there was no more to do or say. She was heard and the storm had lifted. It was over. And the little girl was gone. All that was left was an empty space, with the imprint of a small body that was now free to run.

I was 20 when I left Chicago. I had an opportunity to leave, and I took it. The hardest part was leaving my brother behind. Perhaps I thought it would just be a short break away from home, but when I left Chicago I would never live there again.

Each time I came back to visit, the face of the neighborhood had changed. They tore down the Terminal Theatre. I used to walk by it and tip my head, way back, just to see the statue of the roaring lion perched on the very top. Seventy-five cents would place me in its magical darkness all day long. I'd stay to see double features over and over again. I'd eat popcorn and candy and run up and down the lavish staircase that led to the balcony and let the big screen swallow me up for five or six hours.

The Terminal Theatre was like a palace and now, like my childhood, it was gone. During my visits, I'd stay with my parents. I wouldn't even call my friends when I came back because I just wanted to be with my brother. We'd take long rides and walk on the lakefront beaches. I'm not even sure what we talked about. I only remember the bellyaching, sidesplitting laughter.

Somehow with laughter I didn't take myself, and everything around me, so seriously. Laughter has saved me. Has held me up and supported me. But still, at times, I must cover up with a warm blanket and sing myself a lullaby.

INLAND

My mother's breasts weren't like mine. Mine were small. She told me to put cotton balls in my bra when I first started to develop. As I got older she said stuffing nylon stockings inside would do the trick. But who was I tricking?

I never let anyone see my naked body. I was too embarrassed and ashamed. I would see my girlfriend's breasts on sleepovers or in school when they changed into their gym clothes. They projected an air of beauty and popularity. Their clothes. Their hair. Cheerleaders. Winning was important to them.

I never thought too much about winning before I started going to a female therapist. She thought a lot about winning, and because I thought she knew what was right for me I started to think about winning too. It became my goal. To try to win at everything. It was a worthless waste of time. Ten years' time. Another way to dress, look, talk, love, think, be. How do I look? I look inadequate. Put makeup on and dress monochromatically. Work harder. Work more. She was exhausted at times from working so hard, and she was the first to tell me that no one worked as hard as she did. I certainly didn't.

I didn't deserve to be tired because I didn't work hard. She worked hard. Face-lifts, tummy tucks, nose jobs, chin implants, face peels, etcetera, etcetera. And I took her advice because I was sure she knew what was right for me. No. Partly. But no. I followed her because I didn't know how to ask myself. I didn't know how to answer myself. I didn't know how to trust myself.

With no second thought I lay on a gurney while anesthesia chilled my veins. "I'm dizzy," I said, before everything went black. There was no pain. Even healing was painless. Taking my stitches out was painless. I looked in the mirror, and for the first time in my life I had regular sized breasts. They were a little too big, but the doctor said they were swollen and it would take three to six months for them to look normal. Normal. I went from never letting anyone see my naked body to showing everyone my breasts.

My therapist wanted to see them before the surgery, but I didn't want to show them to her. Though she asked more than once, I held my ground—but after the surgery I proudly lifted my blouse. All she seemed concerned about were if mine were bigger than hers. Then she concluded that they were about the same size. She was satisfied. She'd won.

I never questioned my decision to get breast implants. I didn't even think about it that much. I never talked about it with anyone, not even with my crazy shrink. I just thought it would make me look and feel better. I thought the costumes that I sang in would look better and that I would look better. That was my reason. Consciously. Sub-consciously, something else was brewing.

I had them for eight years. During that entire time I never felt they were mine. I was disconnected from them. They were these things sitting on my chest. Kind of like I was wearing the implants. Or maybe the implants were wearing me. I didn't change my style of dressing either. I thought I would wear more revealing and seductive clothing. I didn't.

My right implant started to harden about a year after the surgery. When people wanted to hug me I would curl my shoulders forward so they wouldn't feel the hardness poking at them. My husband never said anything about it.

The voice inside never lies. The voice tells me who I am. I can pretend and alter the packaging, but I can't change the truth. Truth is always forgiving. But what truth do implants hide? What's to hide?

My body wouldn't live with the lie anymore. It knocked me down. Drained me. No life energy. Exhaustion. The Epstein-Barr blues. Immune system malfunction. My body said, "Stop being who you are *not!* And if you won't stop it, then I will stop you." And it did. Bam! Priority time.

Your health doesn't care about how you look, or if your breasts are big or small. I dragged myself around from doctor to doctor taking test after test, waiting for answers. Never once thought to ask myself.

Most medical professionals deal with science. Holistic health deals with intuitive science. Like intuition. Insight. Knowing. Listening. Shhhhh. Listen. To what? To whatever's going on inside. For a while I moaned and groaned. Whined and complained. But the fatigue didn't lighten. Then I got scared. I wondered if the rest of my life was going to be this way. Forever.

I was too tired to cook a meal, sing a note, have a conversation, be a wife and mother, let alone have a career. Why would anyone want to be with me when I had absolutely nothing to offer? When I was just a complaining, frightened, worried, negative blob of flesh with plastic tits.

It got worse. I was dizzy. Spinning all the time. I was nauseous. Threw up nightly. A wave of nausea would wake me in the middle of the night, and I would bring my pillow and blanket into the bathroom, hang my head in the toilet and sleep on the floor between bouts.

I lost weight. My legs constantly ached. I couldn't get warm. My bones felt as if they were made out of ice. I was depressed and too tired to cry. I felt handicapped. On the days I felt strong enough to go outside, I would look for parking spaces as close as possible to where I was going, and if I couldn't find one I would go home. I had no memory. Was in a mental fog all the time. I felt as if I were dying. Without energy there is no life. I had no energy. I was pale and tired. I didn't look good. My tits looked great.

It was relentless. I would wake up in the morning feeling exhausted. Like I hadn't slept at all. No one was helping me. Medical doctors didn't have anything to give me except pills for nausea. Pills for depression. Pills for dizziness. Intravenous antibiotics. Test after test. I was sure I had cancer and they just couldn't find it.

Then I started going to nutritionists and alternative medical professionals who suggested IVs of vitamin C, herbs, homeopathic remedies, Bach flowers, Candida diets, supplements, vitamins, minerals. I was willing to try anything. I was afraid all the time, and couldn't accept that, out of all the doctors I was seeing, no one was helping me.

It got worse. Smells began to bother me. Any smell. Perfume, deodorant, skin lotion, shampoo, soap, cleaning products, wood, air fresheners, paint, flowers. Everything. Anything. Then, one of the witch doctors who was working with the magnetic fields in my body said that I only needed one thing. Silicon.

My eyes lifted. I understood that the concept of this kind of treatment was to give the patient minuscule doses of whatever was causing their illness. The same premise as a vaccine. Of all the zillions of choices in the world that were available to him, he chose silicon. I had never told him about the implants unless, of course, he had X-ray vision, which at that point in time wouldn't have surprised me at all.

I was sick. Sick of doctors. Sick of fear. Sick of being sick. I stopped going to doctors. I started biofeedback and visualization. It helped calm me down. I liked it. I would usually fall asleep during my treatments, but it was a different kind of sleep. Not as frenetic as my usual dream state. I did it at home regularly.

Then I read a book that talked about getting in touch with your intuitive self. I did all the meditations. I started to hear the voice inside myself. At first in whispers. I did whatever it told me to do. Even if it didn't make any sense to me.

If I felt like eating chicken, I would check with it first. If it said no, I would change to something else. It didn't want me to eat in restaurants. It took care of me. Told me to take naps. Told me to take care of myself. I listened. It got louder. It told me who to talk to and when to hang up the telephone. It made me aware of people's intentions. It only answered if I asked. I never asked about the implants. I was too afraid of the answer.

I started seeing a doctor that I had heard about for over 10 years. He lived five minutes from my home. He was a chiropractor, but his reputation was that of a healer. On the day of my first appointment he came into the room and I backed away from him. He stopped and watched me as I spoke. I told him that if his treatment involved taking anything, or fasting, or chiropractic adjustments, or anything in general, he should tell me immediately so that we don't waste each other's time. I told him that everything made me sick, and that I wasn't going to take anything. He wanted to muscle test me. I knew about kinesiology and I allowed it.

When I left his office, on the way to my car, a strange silence filled me. A quiet. It was coming from the core of my being. It was powerful and engulfed me. I sat in my car waiting for it to go away. It didn't. It never has totally gone away. It was the beginning of a profound feeling. It was hope.

I began seeing this doctor regularly, and became actively involved in my own healing. It took great patience. It was a new world that I knew absolutely nothing about. He confirmed, like the others, that I had Epstein-Barr virus, but he added that I seemed to be in an autoimmune mode, which meant that I was becoming allergic and sensitive to everything around me. Including myself.

He suggested that I remove all of the silver fillings from my teeth. They were weakening my immune system and making me react to electrical frequencies. Oh no. Not that. Anything but the dreaded dentist. It took me a year to muster the courage to start that procedure.

It took eight months, two root canals and two extractions to finish. It was terrifying and exhausting. I was told that I wouldn't feel the benefits until the last silver filling was out. I walked around in a total fog, sometimes sobbing when the appointments were over. It was grueling and painful. It felt like I was being tortured. Finally, the day came for my last appointment. When he finished, it seemed as if someone had washed my eyes. Everything was sharp and clear.

I felt significantly better after I had the fillings removed. My immune system seemed to be stronger, but it wasn't over yet. It's an ongoing process that has taken years, and has led me to one place. Myself. Trusting the voice inside over all others. But my insecurities get the best of me, and sometimes I get separated from it. I can't hear it at all when I'm afraid.

The news started. Women were talking about how they were relating their deteriorating health problems to their breast implants. I called the surgeon who had put mine in, and he told me not to worry. He said that these were probably hysterical, neurotic women who needed to place blame on something for their problems. He told me to wait until there was more information.

I waited. Months passed. I was washing the dishes while the television was on, and heard a woman say, "Autoimmune disease." I turned my head to look at the screen and saw a breast implant sitting on a desk.

I made an appointment to see my surgeon. "What's going on?" I asked. He calmed me down by saying that I had the best implants money could buy from Dow Corning, and the women who were sick had implants coated with polyurethane. "Don't worry," he said. "Wait the 45 days for the panel to present their findings. Then we'll talk. Okay?"

I went home. I asked my voice. "Should I take the implants out?" The voice answered, "*ABSOLUTELY.*" I called the surgeon and told him that I didn't really care what the panel said after the 45-day moratorium. I wanted them out of my body as soon as possible, and I wanted to have the operation without anesthesia.

I was more afraid of the side effects of the anesthesia than I was of the operation itself. I had spent so many nights throwing up from this sickness. It had been a while since the last time I had thrown up, and I knew that vomiting was a side effect of anesthesia. I was still so sensitive to everything, I just couldn't face reliving those awful memories.

The surgeon told me that the last time he operated on anyone without anesthesia was 20 years ago in medical school but he was willing to try. He said that he would use Marcaine, a localized, long-lasting Lidocaine, to numb the breast, but he also wanted a backup to knock me out in case I couldn't handle the pain. I agreed.

I spoke to the anesthesiologist about the backup. He said nitrous oxide doesn't go into the system, because you breathe it in, and once you breathe it out it's gone. All the others would have to be administered with an IV, and would go into my system, and dizziness, nausea, and vomiting were the side effects. The surgeon and the anesthesiologist both thought that I should go with the nitrous oxide. My alternative doctor gave me his approval as well.

Three days before the surgery, I spoke to another doctor, a medical doctor who uses holistic as well as conventional methods, just to get his opinion on the anesthesia. He told me that it would be better to wait until summer to do the surgery because, holistically speaking, people do better in summer. He also asked if I were absolutely positive that my body wanted the surgery. He said, "Do you *really* want the implants out, or do you *think* you want the implants out?"

I was a nervous wreck. When I got home I meditated to calm down and to get in touch with my voice. I asked if I should wait till the summer to take out the implants. My voice shouted, "*NO.*" I then asked if my body *really* wanted the implants out. My voice answered, "*DEFINITELY.*"

The morning of my surgery was very difficult. I tried hard to keep my focus. I moved slowly, and breathed deeply. My husband was there with his love and support, and was very sensitive to my fear. I didn't talk much. The anesthesiologist came into the office to go over the whole procedure one more time. I brought a music cassette of one of my favorite jazz albums, and before I went into the operating room I flashed my breasts at my husband and said, "Say goodbye, honey." His sweet smile calmed me.

I was in the operating room with the surgeon, the anesthesiologist and a nurse. I was on my back, covered with a blanket. My music was playing in the background. The anesthesiologist handed me the mask for the nitrous oxide, and told me to just pull it away from my face when I'd had enough. I was in total control. I was supposed to breathe the gas in for about one minute and then we would begin.

Three breaths. Three lousy breaths. That's all I could handle before I sat straight up, as white as a ghost. "I don't like this feeling! It's making me dizzy, and I don't like this feeling!" I said.

The surgeon backed away from the table. My head was swimming. I thought, "Oh my God, there goes the plan! *WE HAVE NO PLAN NOW!* Maybe I should wait till summer or maybe I should take the backup IV. I'm so nervous I just want to go home." I was in a state of complete panic. "What are we going to do now?" I cried. The surgeon's words calmed my hysteria. He simply said, "Let's take it one step at a time and see how you do." Right. That sounded right. Okay. Let's do it.

First, he put in the IV line. It wasn't exactly fun but I certainly didn't need to be nitrous oxided out for it. My body started to shake uncontrollably. I asked for more covers. Then, he said the next step would be the most horrible thing he could imagine doing to a woman. Great. What exactly would that be? "I'm going to stick your nipple with about six shots of Marcaine. *THIS IS GOING TO HURT.*"

I automatically went into my Lamaze breathing from when I had our daughter. Yeah, I'd had natural childbirth, for God's sake! And root canals too! I tried to remember that I had experienced my share of physical pain and had survived. He injected both breasts, one after the other, so that he could get what he thought was the worst part over with. Again, it wasn't enough to be knocked out for. The anesthesiologist was very encouraging and supportive. He cheered me on all the way.

The surgeon made the incision. I didn't feel a thing. If he thought the injections were the worst part then, as far as I was concerned, I was home free. I started to relax but my body still shook. He started pushing and pulling on my chest. I asked the surgeon to keep talking to me so that I would know what to expect. He said that he wasn't used to talking to his patients while he was operating on them. I had to keep reminding him.

I only felt pressure. No pain. The right one was out. The right side of my chest felt so light. I was acutely aware of the heavy mound on my left side. I wanted it out. One down and one to go. The left one broke on its way out. But not in me. It broke in his hand. They were out of my body. My entire chest felt light again. Normal. My normal. There was one more step to go.

The body naturally forms scar tissue around the implants once they're in. That's what the hardness was, scar tissue to protect me. Protect me from what? From the implant. If the implants are so safe, then why does the body naturally grow this hard, gristly substance around them? It's the body's defense. Against what?

For eight years this hard stuff was there. It was what made me curl my shoulders forward when people hugged me. It was the reason that I had to squeeze my breasts nightly to try to soften them. It was why people took them out and put them in, again and again, hoping that the next operation would make softer scar tissue.

I didn't have more than one operation because, by the time my right breast hardened, I was already showing signs of debilitating health. I was too afraid to put my body through the rigors of another operation and anesthesia, but now I felt healthy enough, and frightened enough by the reports, to have this final surgery.

Ouch. I felt something. He was cutting the scar tissue from my chest wall. He dripped more Marcaine directly onto where he was cutting, but I still felt it. It hurt. I started doing Lamaze breathing again. The anesthesiologist comforted me with encouraging words, but this was really getting painful. I felt him tearing and cutting. I was on that thin line of pain tolerance and intolerance.

It took 25 minutes to remove all the scar tissue from the right breast. I was exhausted. My stomach muscles were killing me from keeping them so tense from the pain. I asked if he really had to cut out the scar tissue from my other breast. He told me that he needed to take all of it out so that it could be sent to the lab to see if any silicone was found in the scar tissue.

I knew that if we took a break I would probably start to cry, and then I would totally lose my focus. My left breast took 20 minutes. I must have asked if he was almost finished at least 400,000 times during those 20 minutes.

Finally, it was over. He was sewing me up. No more pain. The anesthesiologist couldn't believe that I had gone through with it. I was elated. I asked if my husband could come in, and when he entered the operating room I could see by his expression that waiting in the outer lobby hadn't been easy for him. We laughed with relief while the doctor prepared the scar tissue for the lab. My husband went over to look. All of their backs were facing me. I had to see what I had been feeling those eight long years and what had just caused me so much pain.

I got up from the table and walked over to where they were standing. When I looked over the surgeon's shoulder he jumped because he wasn't used to his patients standing up after surgery. I looked at the scar tissue. This shiny, pinkish, tough, smooth, rubbery mass lay on the table. Enough to fill both of my open hands. I felt as though I were looking at the enemy.

I said, "I'm going to get dressed and leave now. Can I please have my music tape?" I was out of there in less than five minutes. We drove home and ate lunch and then went to my doctor/healer to have him check me for infection or for anything that could be a potential problem. I was fine. My body was in shock, but that would just take time to get over. I cried that night when my daughter asked about the surgery. Reliving the painful part made me cry, and I didn't stop for about 15 minutes, but it was over. Over and done with.

And now life continues to take me on its journey, and I go willingly with fear and laughter, dread and joy. And I listen. Closely. I want to live from the center of my being. Sink my teeth into life and savor its juices. Whether bitter or sweet. It's mine. Like my tits. Mine.

Where is home? Mine is in my husband's arms. But sometimes I miss Chicago so much that I think I can smell the spring cut grass and see the wind blowing billowing clouds across the bluest sky. It's the only place where I really know what direction I'm facing at any given time. The empty prairie lots, the tree-lined blocks, the parks, the green, green grass, catching dandelion fuzz as it blows by. The "el" trains and fire escapes. Porches and alleys. The wind and that Midwestern light. Yes. I miss all of that (And after all these years away).

It's like Paul Gauguin's last painting. He left France and his entire family to go to Tahiti to fulfill his lifelong dream — to paint. The Polynesian sun broiled as he was dying of syphilis, living by the aqua-blue sea that surrounded him for years on that hot, humid, tropical island. Yet his dying vision, his last legacy on canvas, is a snow-covered winter French landscape. Now, I ask you, what does that say about home?

THE END

Lani Hall Alpert was born in Chicago, Illinois, and has been a professional vocalist and lyricist since age 19. She traveled the world as a performer, beginning as lead singer, for 5 years, with Sergio Mendes' breakthrough group, Brasil '66, and went on to record 12 solo albums in 3 different languages (English, Porguguese, and Spanish). She sang the title song for the James Bond film, *Never Say Never Again,* starring Sean Connery, and in 1985 Hall won a Grammy award for her Latin CD, *Es Facil Amar.* Lani has also recorded an additional 2 CDs with her musician husband, Herb Alpert.

Spending her professional life as a singer and her private life as a writer, Lani began writing at an early age and penned many lyrics scattered throughout her recording career. This volume is her first book of short stories. Written over a 30 year period, *Emotional Memoirs & Short Stories* is a combining of fiction and non-fiction, uniquely tied together by a personal narrative.

Lani lives in Southern California with her husband of 38 years, Herb Alpert, and has 3 children and 5 grandchildren.

Made in the USA
Charleston, SC
23 October 2013